ANGLICAN–METHODIST UNITY
THE SCHEME

Anglican–Methodist Unity

REPORT
OF THE ANGLICAN–METHODIST
UNITY COMMISSION

Part 2
The Scheme

LONDON
S·P·C·K
AND
THE EPWORTH PRESS
1968

First published in 1968
by S.P.C.K.
Holy Trinity Church
Marylebone Road
London N.W. 1
and
The Epworth Press
25–35 City Road
London E.C. 1

©

SBN 281 02254 2 (S.P.C.K.)
7162 0006 6 (Epworth)

Printed in Great Britain
at the University Printing House, Cambridge

Contents

ACKNOWLEDGEMENTS *page* vii

MEMBERS OF THE COMMISSION ix

ABBREVIATIONS xiii

1 INTRODUCTION 1

2 THE GOAL: ONE CHURCH UNITED FOR MISSION AND SERVICE 6

3 AGREEMENT IN DOCTRINE 10
APPENDIX:
Doctrinal Statements 18
 I Scripture and Tradition 18
 II Priesthood and Ministry 23
 III The Doctrine of Holy Communion: Sacrificial Aspects 30

4 WHY TWO STAGES? 34

5 METHODIST BISHOPS 36

6 ONE ORDINAL FOR BOTH CHURCHES 43
APPENDIX:
Part of the Preface to the Draft Ordinal 46

7 FUTURE RELATIONS WITH OTHER CHURCHES 49

8 NON-PARTICIPATION IN THE SERVICES OF RECONCILIATION 55

9 GROWING TOGETHER IN STAGE ONE 58
APPENDIX:
The Diaconate 65

10 LAY MINISTRIES 67

11 BAPTISM AND CONFIRMATION 74

12 THE CHURCHES AND MARRIAGE 83

13 MATTERS FOR SETTLEMENT DURING STAGE ONE 87

v

CONTENTS

14 JOINT TRAINING FOR THE MINISTRY *page* 90

15 CHURCH, COMMUNITY, AND STATE 92

16 LEGAL ISSUES 100
ANNEXE:
The Draft of the Bill 103
Notes on the Draft Bill 110

17 THE POSITION IN WALES 114

18 THE POSITION IN SCOTLAND 117

19 THE WAY OF RECONCILIATION 120

20 THEOLOGICAL OBJECTIONS 128

21 PRACTICAL OBJECTIONS 136

22 ALTERNATIVES 140

23 THE ACTS OF RECONCILIATION 146

TERMS OF REFERENCE 179

TO OUR CHURCHES 181

A NOTE BY THE REVEREND DR J. I. PACKER 182

INDEX 185

Acknowledgements

The Book of Common Prayer of 1662 is Crown Copyright; extracts herein are used with permission.

Biblical quotations from the *Revised Standard Version* of the Bible, copyrighted 1946 and 1952 by the Division of Christian Education of the National Council of the Churches of Christ in the United States of America, are used by permission.

Biblical quotations from *The New English Bible, New Testament*, copyrighted 1961 by Oxford and Cambridge University Presses, are used by permission.

Members of the Commission

Church of England representatives appointed by the Archbishops of Canterbury and York at the request of the Convocations

The Right Reverend Robert Stopford, D.D. *Chairman*
Bishop of London

The Right Reverend Harry Carpenter, D.D.
Bishop of Oxford

The Right Reverend Gordon Savage
Bishop of Southwell

The Reverend Canon E. W. Kemp, D.D.
Fellow and Chaplain of Exeter College, Oxford

The Reverend J. I. Packer, D.Phil.
Warden of Latimer House, Oxford

The Reverend Prebendary G. B. Timms
Vicar of St Andrew's, Holborn Circus

The Very Reverend Lionel du Toit
Dean of Carlisle

The Very Reverend Robin Woods
Dean of Windsor

Mr C. G. Bridge
Member of the House of Laity of the Church Assembly

Mrs Mark Hodson

Mr T. A. R. Levett
Vice-Chairman of the House of Laity of the Church Assembly

*The Right Honourable R. F. Wood, M.P.

* Mr Wood withdrew in 1966 owing to pressure of parliamentary duties.

Appointed by the Episcopal Church in Scotland

The Right Reverend Richard Wimbush
Bishop of Argyll and the Isles

Appointed by the Church in Wales

The Right Reverend David Bartlett, D.D.
Bishop of St Asaph

Representatives of the Methodist Church appointed by Conference

The Reverend Dr Harold Roberts *Chairman*
Principal of Richmond College, Surrey; President of the Conference 1957

The Reverend Geoffrey J. Ainger
Member of the Notting Hill Team Ministry

The Reverend Dr Eric W. Baker
Secretary of the Conference; President of the Conference 1959

The Reverend Howard A. G. Belben
Principal of Cliff College, Calver, Sheffield

Mr John C. Blake
Vice-President Designate of the Conference 1968

The Reverend Rupert E. Davies
Principal, Wesley College, Bristol

The Reverend Dr Leslie Davison
General Secretary of the Home Mission Department; President of the Conference 1962

The Reverend Thomas Lee
Superintendent of the Moseley Road and Sparkhill Circuit, Birmingham

The Reverend A. Kingsley Lloyd
Secretary of the Department of Connexional Funds; President of the Conference 1964

The Reverend W. Oliver Phillipson
Formerly General Secretary of the Department of Chapel Affairs

The Reverend Edward Rogers
General Secretary of the Department of Christian Citizenship; President of the Conference 1960

The Reverend Griffith T. Roberts
Chairman of the Second North Wales District

The Reverend Frederick A. Rowe
Chairman of the Scotland District

Mr Philip H. Race
Vice-President of the Conference 1957

Miss Pauline M. Webb
Vice-President of the Conference 1965

Secretariat

JOINT SECRETARIES OF THE COMMISSION
The Reverend Dr Eric W. Baker
The Very Reverend Robin Woods

JOINT EXECUTIVE SECRETARIES OF THE COMMISSION
Mr John C. Blake
The Reverend Peter Morgan

everywhere and the new interest in flowers is to arrange them to give an effect of violence, of activity, of strangeness. Gradually that is producing its own elegance.

I was talking to Madame Giroud, she remembers everything and I asked her what seemed to her the most startling difference between the France of her youth the Nineteenth century and the France of to-day. She said undoubtedly the difference in dress of the people living not in cities but in the country. Not alone the girls but the women in villages and country towns all dress well, all clean themselves very much more.

I know that I was much taken with the short sleeves short dresses as being an enormous incentive to personal cleanliness. There was a very great difference between before and after the war about that. It was true of the younger women and even true of the older women.

On the other hand except the introduction of electric light the inside of the houses in the villages and in the country have not changed much. Of course the existence of electric light in itself made things different because any one can see everything more clearly. Then young men have changed and are athletic and clean but as they grow older they tend to be more as they were. The women keep up the standard and that has its great influence upon the children. The men less. I am now speaking of the country and not of the cities. One of the most important things in the city was the introduction of central heating. The houses the shops in Paris and in the other large cities suddenly became very hot. That had to do naturally with the change in fashion of the women the short sleeves the short skirts the lack of underclothes the thinness of the stockings, and as France makes the fashions for everybody the central heating created in the cities in France made the styles. The styles went with the Americanisation of Europe so pronounced immediately after the war, hygienes, bath-tubs, and sport.

Later on and until just now there have been persistent attempts to get back or forward to styles that cover more, and until now they have been resisted because the conditions that produced the post-war fashions more or less persisted. Gradually though the desire to spend money slackened, it was more difficult to make money and therefore there began a tendency to save it. In the old nineteenth century France you were always supposed to live on your last year's income never on your current income. And now every one was living in France on this year's income or next year's income, they were living on the instalment plan, in short they were not being themselves. And slowly they were beginning resenting this tendency, it came from all classes this resistance and the fashions went with it the effort to re-establish more covering to the body longer skirts more durable clothes.

Now there is war, the houses in Paris are not centrally heated any more. In many apartment houses you heat yourself as you can. Many people like ourselves are staying in the country with the boulets fire of France which I have not seen since 1900 and wood fires to help and naturally woollen stockings and other things accompany this and fashions are changing. The darkness has a great deal to do with everything. Madame Giroud always tells me you do not know what these villages were in the old days and even now although the roads are dark the houses and the barns are lighted electrically inside, all the streets are dark but the shops are bright inside. So although they look mediæval outside they do not feel mediæval inside. So even when it is black outside in the twentieth century it is brightly lighted inside. Which was not true of the nineteenth century.

The boulets fires of France the round walnuts of pressed coal that were in all houses in the beginning of the twentieth century quite entirely ceased to exist even in the country, the grates that were put in to the fireplace and balanced by a bit of brick and filled with the walnut coal that gave out a steady small heat and never really seemed to change night or day were not seen any more. And now there is 1939 and war and everybody wants their boulets fire back again. We have one. We found the grates still in the local shops with the same curly design as one we found in the garret of this house which dates from we do not know when. Those in the shops are of exactly the same design which shows how dead boulets fires had been.

And so a century is made of one hundred years and a hundred years is not so long. Anybody can know somebody who remembers somebody else and makes it go back one hundred years. If it cannot be done in two generations it can be done easily done in three. And so one hundred years is not so long.

It is rather a worry that our civilisation if you think of it in the form of three generations making a century does not take many generations to begin.

A century is one hundred years. Every century has a beginning and a middle and an ending. Every century is like the life of any one, the life of any nation, that is to say it begins that is it has a childhood

9 What is true of Asia and Africa is true also of Britain. Since the Conversations began more than twelve years ago, more and more evidence has accumulated that our disunity hampers the mission of the Church, and in some areas has helped to bring it to a halt. This is widely recognized, and nearly all major enterprises in evangelism are now carried out on an ecumenical basis. But those who take part in them find in due course that they cannot share in the sacrament of Holy Communion, except on special occasions, and those who are influenced by them are in the same position. The result is often frustration, impatience, and the gradual cessation of effort. In new housing areas many schemes of co-operation are being carried out; but at a certain point in the development of these schemes Christians find that they are unable to share a full sacramental life and to do together the other things which union would make possible. This causes deep disappointment, and a halt is often called to further advance. In the 'People Next Door' campaign, as in other inter-denominational projects, it was found repeatedly that those who had worked closely together in mission reached a stage of co-operation beyond which they found they could not go, though they longed to do so, while their Churches remained disunited.

10 Few will doubt that one cause of the continued decline in the influence and numerical strength of the Churches of this country is their disunity. There is also a serious decline, in large sections of both Churches, in the number of men offering for the ordained ministry. There is good reason to think that in many cases men who would otherwise have offered themselves have refused to enter the ministry of their Churches because of the pattern of incompetence which they present in which disunity is a main feature.

11 Meanwhile, groups of younger Christians of every denomination are beginning to feel that the prolonged discussions of the problems of unity are irrelevant to their concerns, and are proposing to strike out independently of their Churches, which have remained content with division for so long. Such a development could only result in greater and graver disunity.

12 In the light of these facts, it may be that some who have genuine reservations about parts of the present scheme will feel that, never-theless, because of the extreme urgency of the Churches' present situation, it must have their support, especially since it is clear, as this Report shows, that no other scheme which is able to gain equal acceptance is in sight. Those who are already convinced that the scheme offers the best way forward will be encouraged to advocate it

the more earnestly because they foresee that, if it is rejected, the cause of unity, and with it the whole mission of the Church, will be set back many years, and perhaps many decades.

13 It has been argued that acceptance of the present scheme by the two Churches will lead to divisions within both of them. However true this may be, it is beyond doubt that its rejection by either Church would lead to very serious cleavages in both of them. A very large number of men and women, ordained and lay, would take such rejection as dashing their hopes for their Church's obedience to the gospel, and in disillusionment might well seek their future elsewhere.

14 Nor will the results of the acceptance or rejection of a plan for union which is already so far advanced be limited to Britain. In Ceylon, North India, Pakistan, Australia, New Zealand, Nigeria, Ghana, and other places, schemes of union are similarly nearing the point of decisive action. It is known that Christians in each of these countries are looking for a lead to be given in Britain, not because this country is more important than others, but because it contains the Mother Church of the world-wide Anglican communion and the Mother Church of the world-wide Methodist communion.

15 If our Churches are seen to be saying 'no' to union in this country, the cause of union overseas, with which the cause of mission is bound up even more intimately than in Britain, will in many places receive a disastrous setback. If, however, our Churches agree together to go on into reconciliation and union, and come to this decision in the near future, it is no exaggeration to say that a series of unions between Churches will be initiated, in this country and elsewhere, which will ultimately spread round the world.

16 We have had constantly in mind the principle that Church relations should not be advanced in one direction in a way which will restrict their advance in another. We deal with this more fully in Chapter 7, but we wish to emphasize here that we believe that the scheme can go forward without endangering the fellowship of the Methodist Church with other Free Churches and World Methodism, or of the Church of England with Churches of a 'Catholic' tradition. We have taken great pains to keep in touch with Roman Catholic, Orthodox, Old Catholic, and Free Church leaders and theologians.

17 The time for negotiation, consultation, and reflection, necessarily protracted, must soon reach its term. The time for decision is upon our Churches.

The Need for a Common Mind

18 We are vividly conscious, however, that, though the need for union is pressing, neither this nor any other union scheme can be carried through successfully without very powerful support from both clergy and laity in the Churches involved. To proceed with plans for union in face of substantial opposition would be intolerable. If our Churches are deeply divided on this matter, either the acceptance or the rejection of the scheme would have tragic consequences. We therefore urge both our Churches to seek by all possible means to achieve a common mind among their members, both ordained and lay.

The Plan of this Report

19 Our Report has a double function to fulfil. On the one hand, it needs to present the scheme as straightforwardly as possible, so that the great body of members of our two Churches may be able to grasp it easily and thus to reach fully responsible decisions about it, based on full understanding of it. On the other hand, great theological issues are at stake, and they must be dealt with sufficiently fully to satisfy all proper concerns about them. It was partly for this reason that the Report was divided into two parts. The revised draft Ordinal was published separately as Part I, because of its intrinsic importance and the concern about the doctrine of the ministry which was evidently widely felt. Part II contains twenty-three chapters of exposition, together with the text of the proposed Services of Reconciliation. These chapters contain a complete review of the scheme, and of the considerations by which, in our judgement, decisions on it should finally be determined.

20 The main constituents of the scheme which these chapters survey are as follows:

(a) Acceptance of organic union as the goal.
(b) The establishing of sufficient doctrinal agreement for union.
(c) Advance into union by two stages.
(d) The taking of the historic episcopate, and a rule of episcopal ordination, into the Methodist Church.
(e) The use of a common Ordinal in both Churches from the start.
(f) The pledge never to jeopardize relations of eucharistic fellowship which either Church now enjoys.
(g) Co-ordination of divergent practices, for growth together during Stage One.
(h) Agreement as to what questions should be left for settlement during Stage One.
(i) A public reconciliation of the two Churches, and integration of their ministries, by means of liturgical services.

5

2 The Goal: One Church United for Mission and Service

Towards Organic Union

21 The first Conversations, which began in 1956, were concerned initially with the establishing of intercommunion on the basis of the Methodist Church taking episcopacy into its system. However, in their Interim Statement, published in 1958, the two conversing committees recorded that: 'In the course of our discussions, we have been led with impressive unanimity to the conviction that nothing short of organic unity, whatever form it may take, should be our final goal' (*IS*, p. 41). The Convocations of Canterbury and York and the Methodist Conference endorsed this conviction, and the 1958 Lambeth Conference gave encouragement to continue the Conversations, 'on the understanding that organic union is definitely accepted as the final goal, and that any plans for the interim stage of intercommunion are definitely linked with provisions for the steady growing together of the Churches concerned' (*The Lambeth Conference 1958*, Resolution 30, p. 1.38).

22 Organic union means full communion within a single organizational fellowship. It implies, not a bare uniformity, but a rich variety of life within a common order. Since 1958, the acceptance of organic union as the end in view has been a fixed point in discussion. The 1963 Report declared: 'If, however, our Churches agree to accept stage one of this movement, we believe that it is essential that they should at the same time accept the obligation to achieve, in due course, union with one another in one Church' (*Report*, p. 9). This acceptance was expressed in the official resolutions of both Churches in 1965, and is part of the basis on which the present Commission was set up. It is doubtful whether the Methodist Church would have agreed in 1965 to accept episcopacy, or would consent to accept it now, if organic union were not the pledged goal.

Practical Arguments for Union

23 Many pragmatic reasons can be given for adhering at the present time to the goal of union. The amount of joint activity in which our

6

two Churches are already engaged makes our separateness appear increasingly anomalous and inconvenient. It is high time to concentrate Christian forces for effective missionary action in our secularized society. Members of our Churches feel further from each other than they really are; separation gives rise to prejudicial images of each other, and so hinders the growth of fellowship. It has become clear that there are no substantial doctrinal issues keeping us apart. Moreover, the move towards union has already begun: in many fields where our two Churches co-operate in pastoral endeavour, local plans formed since 1965 have been based on the assumption that union is coming within the foreseeable future. To go back on this at the present time would be a major disaster, not merely for the cause of unity, but for the Christian mission itself.

Unity must be made Visible

24 Weighty as these considerations are, however, the grounds of principle dictating the pursuit of organic union are even stronger. The main reasons for making organic union the goal, and viewing full communion—that is, free interchange of communicants and ministers—as a stage in the progress towards it, are not, and never were, pragmatic: they are biblical and theological.

25 As the 1958 Interim Statement said: 'The Church is the People of God, and is one since God is One. All members of the Church have a hidden unity with one another through their common relation to Christ. But the Church is also visible in the world as an organized society, and its visible form ought not to contradict its hidden nature but should make it manifest as far as may be' (p. 18). The New Testament knows nothing of a Church which, though spiritually united, is outwardly split into dissociated groups of congregations, such as our denominations are. The unity of the Church in the New Testament is both spiritual and visible, and should be equally visible in every age.

26 To stress the importance of visible unity in this way is not to lose sight of, nor to undervalue, the inward, spiritual unity of the People of God. This God-given spiritual unity is primary and fundamental: no one questions that. Nor does the stress on visible unity imply that, without organizational oneness, the prior spiritual unity of the People of God altogether lacks manifestation. By a common profession of the Christian faith, and a common baptism in the Triune Name of God, separated Christian bodies are already manifesting their given unity in some measure. But this fact, far from relieving Churches of the

7

obligation to manifest unity with each other at every level in their common life, only makes this obligation clearer, and neglect of it more of a scandal.

27 The manifesting of unity today calls for the setting up of synodical and organizational links between our two geographically overlapping communities, and for the removal of the anomaly whereby adjacent congregations look for fellowship primarily to local churches of their own denominational type elsewhere, rather than to their geographical neighbours. In any case, a full sharing of Christian life, witness, and enterprise can exist only where organizational connections are formed; full communion alone cannot achieve it. It is obligatory, therefore, for our two Churches to seek organic union.

Episcopacy and Union

28 Moreover, the establishing of full communion between our two Churches, as now proposed, is to be linked with Methodist acceptance of the historic episcopate 'as a sign and token of the unity and continuity of the Church of Jesus Christ' (*TR*, p. 16), and this acknowledged meaning of episcopacy makes the prospect of indefinitely continuing parallel episcopates appear as an intolerable anomaly. It could not be right for the Methodist Church to 'take episcopacy into its system' save on the basis of a firm resolve that the Anglican and Methodist episcopates should become one, through the union of our two Churches, as soon as possible.

God's Call to Action

29 As we said in *Towards Reconciliation* (p. 5), we are conscious that since the 1963 Report appeared 'the momentum of ecumenical progress has strikingly increased'. Whether or not the suggestion of the 1964 Nottingham Conference, that the member Churches of the British Council of Churches should covenant together to achieve organic union on a stated date, and that this date should be Easter 1980, is finally acted on, the fact that it was made at all is one more proof of this. Impatience to be rid of our inherited divisions, for the sake of more effective evangelism, and a willingness to contemplate costly change and upheaval to this end, is becoming more and more evident among younger Christian people, both ordained and lay. We wish to record our firm conviction that what these facts mean is that God is pressing on the consciences of his people his call to them to manifest a new obedience to revealed truth in organic union and

8

witness to Christ, as an immediate task. We feel bound to record also that the arguments we have heard for not planning beyond Stage One, or even for postponing the whole scheme indefinitely, seem to lack the clear basis in scriptural theology which this call to unity has.

The Hope of Wider Union

30   It may be asked why, if the goal is the reunion of the whole divided Church in this country, the Church of England and the Methodist Church should be negotiating together, without other Churches being directly involved. The answer to this question is historical: in 1955, of the Free Churches represented in the earlier talks which produced the report *Church Relations in England*, only the Methodist Church responded to the invitation to enter into conversations with the Church of England with a view to establishing closer relations. Recent events, however, make us bold to hope that relationships with other Churches may so develop during Stage One that Stage Two may be a multilateral union. What advances may become possible in relations with other Churches not yet directly involved in union negotiations, we cannot foretell, though developments in the last few years, especially since the Second Vatican Council, open up possibilities undreamed of a generation ago. Suffice it to say that one Church renewed for mission, in England as elsewhere, must be our goal.

3 Agreement in Doctrine

The Need for Doctrinal Assurances

31 Anglican–Methodist Conversations were inaugurated on the basis of the findings of the report, *Church Relations in England*, produced in 1950 by representatives of the Church of England and the member Churches of the Free Church Federal Council. Discussing 'requirements on either side for the acceptance of some measure of intercommunion' between the Church of England and any Free Church, that report first stressed the need for mutual doctrinal assurances.

> Assurances with respect to doctrinal standards having been mutually exchanged, each Church would declare itself satisfied that the other maintained the apostolic faith and proclaimed the apostolic gospel...
>
> Those engaged in these Conversations are agreed that such 'assurances with respect to doctrinal standards' would be based on the conviction that 'the Holy Scriptures contain sufficiently all doctrine required of necessity for eternal salvation through faith in Jesus Christ'.
>
> This conviction is regarded by the Conference as essential to any attempt to develop closer relations between our various Churches. (*CRE*, pp. 43 f.)

32 Accordingly, the doctrine of our two Churches has been one major subject of discussion throughout. This discussion has reflected an awareness of the distinction between what a Church confesses and defines, on the one hand, and what latitude of opinion it tolerates, on the other. It has been recognized that neither Church's doctrinal position can be fairly assessed without considering both these issues.

The Sources of Doctrine

33 So far as official standards are concerned, the doctrine of the Church of England is set forth particularly in its legally authorized formularies, the Thirty-nine Articles and the Book of Common Prayer, together with the Ordinal. The doctrinal position of the Methodist Church is indicated in general terms in clause 30 of the Deed of Union, and more fully in statements on particular issues

which the Methodist Conference, in its constitutional function as interpreter of Methodist doctrine, has made from time to time.[1]

The Doctrinal Statements in 'Towards Reconciliation'

34 In both Churches, however, the present range of theological opinion, developed in each case with an unquestionable intention of loyalty to the formularies, is wide, and it is not easy to describe it without making it seem wider than it is. The doctrinal statements in *Towards Reconciliation*, which, in response to requests for clarification, indicated the width of the spectrum of conflicting expositions of certain themes, appear to have occasioned some anxiety on this score. Three facts about these statements must, however, constantly be borne in mind.

35 First, their content was determined by their purpose. They were drawn up 'to provide a factual basis for resolving the question whether we hold enough in common to warrant advance into full communion, and ultimately union, *despite differences of belief which remain at present unresolved*' (*TR*, p. 3). This explains why at that point in our discussions it was necessary to highlight the differences. It was not suggested that doctrinal matters are of no importance, or that members of our Churches are encouraged to hold any belief they prefer, without regard to the teaching expressed in the formularies and historic practice of their Church.

36 Second, these statements were produced against the background of a wide area of doctrinal agreement already established. Earlier statements had already borne witness to this. Thus, *Church Relations in England* had declared:

> On the doctrines of God the Father, the Person and Work of Christ, the Person and mission of the Holy Spirit, the Trinity, and the Life Everlasting we have found nothing which separates any one of these

[1] These are: *The Nature of the Christian Church* (1937); *Statement on Holy Baptism* (1952); *Ordination in the Methodist Church* (1960); *Church Membership* (1961). With these should be linked the Junior and Senior Catechisms, approved by the Conference in 1951 and 1952 respectively.

The status given by clause 30 of the Deed of Union to John Wesley's *Notes on the New Testament* and his *44 Standard Sermons* should be noticed. They are declared to contain the 'Evangelical Doctrines to which the preachers of the Methodist Church both Ministers and Laymen are pledged'. However, they 'are not intended to impose a system of formal or speculative theology on Methodist Preachers but to set up standards of preaching and belief which should ensure loyalty to the fundamental truths of the Gospel of Redemption and ensure the continued witness of the Church to the realities of the Christian experience of salvation'.

Communions from another. All acknowledge the apostolic faith as contained in the Scriptures and expressed in the Apostles' and Nicene Creeds (*CRE*, p. 26).

Similarly, the 1958 Interim Statement devotes its first major chapter (Chapter 2) to exhibiting 'an existing unity in Christian faith and purpose' which already binds our two Churches together (p. 5). It insists that a pre-condition of closer communion through Methodist acceptance of episcopacy must be 'mutual assurance of agreement in matters of fundamental doctrine, including the apostolic faith as contained in the scriptures and expressed in the Apostles' Creed and the Nicene Creed, and on the necessity of the sacraments of Holy Baptism and Holy Communion'. Then it goes on to say: 'From our survey of the common ground between our Churches (see Chapter 2) we are confident that the requisite assurances could be given and accepted' (p. 38).

37   Third, the doctrinal statements in *Towards Reconciliation* indicate that doctrinal differences do not follow denominational lines, but rather cut across them, since the differences of view set out there are to be found *within* both Churches. This fact in itself is a reason why it can be asserted without reservation that enough doctrinal agreement exists to warrant advance into organic union. The spectrum of doctrinal differences is not likely to be wider in a united Church than it is already in our separate Churches. We recognize that this is not always apparent in local situations, or to those who cherish particular points of view within our present Churches; none the less, we have reached the considered conclusion that it is an accurate statement of fact.

38   We believe that study of the doctrinal material which we and our predecessors have submitted in the 1958 Interim Statement, the 1963 Report, *Towards Reconciliation*, and the present Report, dealing in particular with the themes of Scripture and tradition, priesthood, episcopacy, and the two dominical sacraments, is of basic importance. Not only, as we believe, does this material warrant 'an affirmative answer' to the question whether, despite our differences, we hold enough in common to go on to organic union (*TR*, p. 3); it also helps to clear away misunderstandings of each other's views which have in the past confused both 'Catholics' and 'Protestants' within our Churches. By showing that our continuing differences exist within, and do not destroy, our common allegiance to the fundamentals of the gospel, this material, we believe, can help to provide a basis for mutual trust and constructive exchanges in the future.

Latitude given for Theological Explorations

39 A further fact to note regarding doctrine in our two Churches is this. Contemporary developments in science and philosophy, together with a widespread secularization of culture, have created new problems for Christian communication to the world and raised new questions about the nature and meaning of Christianity itself. Without loosening hold of any part of the faith stated in their formularies, both our Churches see cause in this situation to give place for free theological exploration of these issues, even in ways which to many of their own members seem unsuccessful. It is important that the motives behind this policy, which correspond in both Churches, should be clearly understood, so as to avoid puzzlement or mistrust on either side.

Fundamental Agreements

40 The contents of this chapter so far have been prompted by particular expressions of anxiety recently voiced. Were no more said, the impression might still be left that confusion and discord are the dominant features of the theological scene both within and between our Churches. Some evidently believe that this is so; mutual suspicion of doctrinal laxity at vital points is sometimes met. Anglicans are found who doubt whether at the level of theology and preaching their Methodist brothers show an adequate grasp of the objective realities of the Trinity and Incarnation, radical human sinfulness, Christ's atonement for sin, pardoning and renewing grace given through word and sacraments, the supernatural character of the Church, and the divine authority of the ordained ministry. Equally, some Methodists suspect that some of their Anglican brothers have too weak a hold on the scriptural realities of the universal free grace of God, personal conversion and new birth, Christian liberty, the life-giving power of the Spirit, fellowship with God through Christ, and the priesthood of all believers.

41 No doubt there have been in the past disparities of statement and emphasis, aggravated by the distorting effect of self-justifying polemics and mismanaged controversy, in both Churches. The course of their history since their separation made that virtually inevitable. But we are convinced that any impression of major doctrinal tension between the two Churches, or of fundamental doctrinal uncertainty in either or both at the present time, would be quite false. As has been said already, our particular differences presuppose wider and more basic agreements at every point, and we are

confident that when in fellowship together some traditional negations and antitheses are re-examined on both sides, a hitherto unsuspected measure of theological harmony will be seen to exist. It is a striking fact that Anglicans and Methodists taking part in ecumenical discussions repeatedly find themselves in substantial doctrinal agreement. We ask that the doctrinal statements from *Towards Reconciliation*, reprinted as Appendixes to this chapter of our Report,[1] should be reviewed specifically from this point of view, together with what is said elsewhere about baptism[2] and the following comments on three further doctrinal matters.

(a) The Place of the Historic Creeds in both Churches

42 The Church of England accepts and upholds the three Creeds, 'for they may be proved by most certain warrants of Holy Scripture' (Article VIII), and the Prayer Book uses all three in worship: the Apostles' Creed in Morning and Evening Prayer and Holy Baptism, the Nicene Creed in Holy Communion, and the Athanasian Creed in place of the Apostles' at Morning Prayer on thirteen days of the year (though this requirement is rarely observed today, except on Trinity Sunday). The 1920 Lambeth Appeal made 'wholehearted acceptance' of the Nicene Creed 'as the sufficient statement of the Christian faith', and of it or the Apostles' Creed as 'the Baptismal confession of belief', a condition of visible unity.

43 Some Anglicans, noting that the 1932 Deed of Union speaks only in general terms of the Methodist Church accepting 'the fundamental principles of the historic creeds', that the Methodist baptismal office contains no creed, and that the authorized Methodist forms of Morning Prayer and Holy Communion (first alternative), in which the Apostles' and Nicene Creeds appear, are not for compulsory use, fear that this reduced stress on the Creeds betokens a loose attitude to their contents. But this fear is certainly groundless. It should be noted that the first section of the Methodist Senior Catechism is an exposition of the Apostles' Creed, fuller than its counterpart in either the Prayer Book Catechism or the Anglican Revised Catechism of 1961. The new Methodist baptismal office contains the Apostles' Creed, and the new form for Holy Communion to be presented to the Conference of 1968 contains the Nicene Creed. The increasing use of set liturgical forms for Sunday worship in Methodist churches will

[1] Scripture and Tradition, Appendix I, pp. 18–22 below; Priesthood and Ministry, Appendix II, pp. 23–9 below; Sacrificial Aspects of Holy Communion, Appendix III, pp. 30–3 below.
[2] Chapter II, pp. 74–82 below.

mean that more and more Methodist worshippers will regularly confess their faith in the words of the Creeds. With this should be linked the fact that some of the weightiest modern elucidations of Trinitarian and Christological doctrine have come from Methodist scholars.[1] There is no warrant whatever for questioning the fullness of the Methodist commitment to the faith of the Catholic Creeds, and every reason to expect that through growth together in Stage One the reality of this commitment will become yet more evident.

(b) The Principles of the Reformation in both Churches

44 The Methodist Deed of Union professes allegiance to 'the fundamental principles of the historic creeds *and of the Protestant Reformation*'. The Methodist Senior Catechism's answer to the question, 'What are the Protestant Churches?' (q. 41), shows what the Methodist Church takes these principles to be. There it is stated: 'Those Churches are called Protestant which have been raised up by God to revive the witness to the supreme authority of the Scriptures, Salvation by Faith, the Priesthood of All Believers, and the Ministry of the Whole Church.'

45 The Catechism has more to say about the second, third, and fourth of these principles. Salvation by Faith is the theme of questions 24–39. Defined in question 26 as 'deliverance from sin into a new life of righteousness that begins on earth, survives death, and is perfected with God in heaven', salvation is analysed in terms of the free and gracious work whereby God 'converts, justifies, regenerates, and sanctifies every repentant sinner who has faith in Jesus Christ crucified for us' (q. 27). It is explained that 'faith in Jesus Christ is trusting in Him alone for salvation' (q. 31), and the work of the Holy Spirit in regeneration, sanctification, and assurance is emphasized. As for the Priesthood of All Believers, question 44 defines it thus: 'All members of the Church share the privilege and responsibility of direct access to God, of bringing others into personal relationship with Him, and of interceding for them.' To the next question, 'What is the Ministry of the Church?', the answer is: 'The ministry of the Church is the continuance of Christ's own ministry through the whole membership of the Church.'

46 Some Methodists, noting that the Prayer Book makes no explicit mention of the priesthood of all believers and the ministry of

[1] For example, A. W. Wainwright, *The Trinity in the New Testament*; V. Taylor, *The Person of Christ in New Testament Teaching*; *The Atonement in New Testament Teaching*.

the whole Church, but centres attention rather on the historic ordained ministry, and knowing that the professed Evangelical school of thought in the Church of England has historically been a minority position, fear that the Anglican tendency will be to smother these historic Methodist emphases. But this fear also is certainly groundless. In the first place, the Reformation doctrine of salvation from sin through the free gift of justification, bestowed by God's grace on the ground of Christ's merit, received 'by Faith only', and issuing in sanctification, holy living, and final glory, is fully stated in IX–XVIII of the XXXIX Articles, and the Prayer Book reflects it throughout. Moreover, modern Anglican theology, as it has come under the influence of the biblical and theological revival which has touched all Christendom in our day, has increasingly endorsed the positive theological thrusts of the Reformation. It is now generally accepted, for instance, that the royal priesthood of all the faithful in Christ is the proper starting-point for all thought about the life, worship, and ministry of the Christian Church, and the concept of 'every man in his ministry' within the Body of Christ is being explored by Anglicans with a new measure of seriousness. Anglicans today are more aware than they once were that they have need to learn from the Reformation heritage of spirituality and ministry, as historic Methodism has developed it, and there is every reason to expect that as the two Churches grow together in Stage One the fruits of this heritage will increasingly appear in the life of the Church of England.

(c) *The Doctrine of the Ministry in both Churches*

47 It is at this point that the traditional emphases of our two Churches are felt to be in the sharpest contrast. The Methodist stress is on the Church as the Spirit-filled community, and on ministering to others as the responsibility of every member—an emphasis in which the origin of Methodism as a religious society is clearly reflected. The Anglican stress is on the historic threefold ministry, representing God to his people in virtue of the commission transmitted in ordination—an emphasis reflecting the Anglican sense of continuity with the catholic visible Church of which the apostles were both founder-members and pioneer ministers. Are these contrasting emphases mutually exclusive? We believe that the statement on the Church and the ministry which now forms the bulk of the Preface to the proposed Ordinal achieves a new degree of synthesis which holds out good hope for future growth together into a common mind, even though, as our statement on Priesthood and Ministry[1] shows, there

---

[1] Appendix II, pp. 23–9 below.

are some continuing antitheses which do not at present appear to admit of resolution. We believe that what the Preface says about (*a*) the Church as the community empowered by Christ's Spirit and charged to continue his mission; (*b*) the priesthood of bishop and presbyter as one form of participation in the royal priesthood which the whole Church has received from Christ; (*c*) the givenness of the ordained ministry, and of its ambassadorial and representative functions; and (*d*) the work of the Holy Spirit in ordination, will have major significance in bridging long-standing theological gaps, and we ask both our Churches to study the statement carefully from this standpoint.[1] We are confident that on this matter, as on the rest of the doctrinal issues that have come before us, sufficient agreement in doctrine to warrant advance towards union is now abundantly plain.

Towards Greater Doctrinal Unity

48   To plan for a union of Churches requires realism; therefore existing doctrinal tensions must be frankly faced. But the goal is unity in truth; therefore our present tensions cannot be accepted as ultimate. In dealing with matters of doctrine, we have sought to keep before us both these principles, and, whereas in *Towards Reconciliation* we emphasized our present incompleteness of agreement on some issues, our stress is now on the hope which we see of wider and deeper agreements being reached as we worship, work, and talk together during Stage One.

[1] See further Chapter 6 on pp. 43–8 below.

APPENDIX:
DOCTRINAL STATEMENTS

I. Scripture and Tradition

Reprinted from Chapter 2 of *Towards Reconciliation*, with further comments.

Aim of this Statement

49 The signatories of the 'Dissentient View',[1] and others in both our Churches, hold that 'the discussion of this fundamentally important subject on pp. 15–19 (of the 1963 Report) does not recognize adequately the pre-eminent and normative place of scripture, or set out satisfactorily its relation to tradition'. In view of this, the Methodist Conference of 1965 asked for 'clarification of Scripture and Tradition in the Report'. The statement that follows has been drawn up to meet this request.

The Supremacy of Scripture

50 The discussion in the 1963 Report contained the following assertions about Scripture and tradition respectively.

Holy Scripture is and must always be the supreme standard of faith and morals in the Church because it embodies the testimony of chosen witnesses to God's saving action. The Old Testament is the prophetic witness of God's people under the old covenant; the New Testament is the apostolic testimony entrusted to the Church under the new. The Church has not made up its gospel from its own experience, but has received it from witnesses, and the Holy Spirit assures us that their witness is true.[2]

Tradition, in the sense of the handing down of the faith from one generation to another, is both inevitable and inescapable. But what is to be handed down, without perversion or addition or alteration, is in the first place the apostolic testimony of scripture. The formulation of the canon is a sufficient sign that the early Church intended to distinguish between the apostolic tradition and all later tradition, and to insist that the apostolic tradition as witness to the work of God in Christ should be the norm of all other tradition.[3]

51 These assertions have the effect of establishing holy Scripture as the sole and authoritative source of 'all doctrine required of necessity to eternal salvation', and as the norm and standard of doctrinal and ethical teaching, of worship, and of practice for the Church in every age.

The Value and Limitations of Tradition

52 The word 'tradition' may denote either (1) the whole process whereby Christianity is handed down in the Church, or (2) the total version of

---

[1] *Report*, pp. 57 ff.   [2] Ibid., p. 15.   [3] Ibid., p. 17.

Christianity which has been transmitted in a particular part of the Church, or (3) an individual item so transmitted. If these distinctions are borne in mind, the import of the following statements on the place and use of tradition becomes clear.

Every tradition, whether of teaching, custom, or institution, will enrich the Church from age to age... just in so far as it witnesses to Christ as the deed of God in the world and as the source and centre alike of Christian faith and Christian community.[1]

This is to say, only items of tradition which express and elucidate the norm—that is, the apostolic witness to Christ, as the New Testament records it—are of value.

Scripture and tradition ought not to be put over against one another. Both are gifts and instruments of the Holy Spirit within the Church. Behind both is the Living Word of God, the Word made flesh in Jesus Christ... We consider this continuing flow of Christian existence from one generation to another [i.e. tradition in sense (1) above], to be of great significance, and it would be intolerable to suppose that it could have come into existence apart from the work of the Holy Spirit.[2]

This is to say that, for example, the writings of the Fathers, the Reformers, the classical Anglican divines, and the Wesleys, the historic Creeds, and the liturgies and formularies of the great communions of Christendom— to name only a few of the forms of 'tradition'—yield many rich insights into the meaning and application of Scripture, which should be thankfully received, as gifts from God.

53 Because tradition, in the sense of the traditionary process, springs from the constant work of the Holy Spirit guiding the Church into all the truth, as it is in Jesus and as the Scriptures set it forth, tradition is indeed 'holy' and to be 'treated with affection and reverence'.[3] It may be rightly called 'the living stream of the Church's life',[4] and the warning that it is 'not to be set aside lightly or unadvisedly'[5] is necessary and important.

54 But, venerable and valuable though it is, tradition in this wider sense 'by itself... exercises no authority, gives no answer to the problem acutely raised in many critical periods of Church history, how to diagnose virus, poison in the blood stream, and what are the remedies and safeguards against it'.[6] Tradition, however high and holy, can never stand by itself. The words of the 'Dissentient View' may here be echoed: 'All Christians have much to learn from the past, but it is their perpetual obligation to bring their inherited customs, institutions and traditions to the bar of Scripture, by which Christ rules his Church.'[7] The products of the traditionary process must be tested by the Scriptures to which they claim to be subservient, and wherever they are found deficient they must be reformed.

[1] *Report*, p. 17.   [2] Ibid., pp. 17 f.   [3] Ibid., p. 18.
[4] Ibid., p. 17.   [5] Ibid., p. 18.   [6] Ibid., p. 18.
[7] Ibid., p. 58.

Anglican and Methodist Formularies

55 The principles that holy Scripture is the supreme and sufficient rule of faith and life, and that ecclesiastical tradition has value, and claims the Christian's allegiance, only so far as it expounds and subserves holy Scripture, are embodied with great clarity in the formularies of both our Churches. On the theme of authority in the Church, the Anglican Articles speak as follows:

> 'Holy Scripture containeth all things necessary to salvation: so that whatsoever is not read therein, nor may be proved thereby, is not to be required of any man, that it should be believed as an article of the Faith, or be thought requisite or necessary to salvation.'[1] The reason why 'the Three Creeds...ought thoroughly to be received and believed' is because 'they may be proved by most certain warrants of Holy Scripture'.[2] Even General Councils 'may err, and sometimes have erred, even in things pertaining unto God. Wherefore things ordained by them as necessary to salvation have neither strength nor authority, unless it may be declared that they be taken out of Holy Scripture.'[3] 'The Church hath power to decree Rites or Ceremonies, and authority in Controversies of Faith: And yet it is not lawful for the Church to ordain any thing that is contrary to God's Word written...'[4] 'It is not necessary that Traditions and Ceremonies be in all places one, and utterly alike...they...may be changed according to the diversities of countries, times, and men's manners, so that nothing be ordained against God's Word.'[5]

The doctrinal clauses in the Deed of Union of the Methodist Church which deal with Methodist standards of faith and life testify to the same basic positions.

> The Methodist Church...rejoices in the inheritance of the Apostolic Faith and loyally accepts the fundamental principles of the historic creeds and of the Protestant Reformation.... The Doctrines of the Evangelical Faith which Methodism has held from the beginning and still holds are based upon the Divine revelation recorded in the Holy Scriptures. The Methodist Church acknowledges this revelation as the supreme rule of faith and practice. These Evangelical Doctrines to which the Preachers of the Methodist Church, both ministers and laymen, are pledged are contained in Wesley's Notes on the New Testament and the first four volumes of his sermons.

These documents 'are not intended to impose a system of formal or speculative theology on Methodist Preachers, but to set up standards of preaching and belief which should secure loyalty to the fundamental truths of the Gospel of Redemption and ensure the continued witness of the Church to the realities of the Christian experience of salvation'.

[1] Article VI. [2] Article VIII. [3] Article XXI.
[4] Article XX. [5] Article XXXIV.

The Nature and Interpretation of the Bible

56 Within this area of common agreement and the limits set by the formularies of the two Churches, there exist differences of opinion and emphasis regarding the nature and interpretation of the Bible. These differences are found in each Church, and in no way follow denominational lines.

57 Some hold that the whole of canonical Scripture, like the teaching given orally by prophets, apostles, and Jesus Christ himself, is inspired in the sense of being a fully human utterance which is just as fully divine. On this view, inspiration is analogous to incarnation, and holy Scripture is both man's witness to God and God's own witness to himself. It is, therefore, wholly trustworthy and free from error in all that it teaches. The Bible's authority is the authority both of God-given truth and of the God of truth himself, who gave it, and who addresses the Church constantly through it. Thus, the Church's task in interpretation is to seek, with the Spirit's help, to elucidate and apply Biblical teaching as truth from God, displaying its inner coherence and subjecting human thoughts and ways wholly to its judgement.

58 Others, while acknowledging that the Bible as a whole is the Word of God, hold that Scripture itself shows signs of more than one kind and degree of inspiration, and that on this basis some writings in both Testaments must be given greater authority than others, as witnessing more directly to the mind and purpose of the Incarnate Lord. Many add that, since the Bible was received from the Lord by the Church, and has been handed down to us by the Church, it is itself the primary form of the Church's tradition. Some would go on to argue that certain developments of this tradition within the New Testament itself need to be modified according to the norm provided by those writings which bear most direct testimony to Christ.

59 Others hold that, since Biblical criticism has disclosed so many possibilities of error in the recording and transmission of Israelite history, prophetic and apostolic teaching, and the words and deeds of Jesus himself, the Church cannot legitimately require belief in more than a limited number of facts held to be basic to God's revelation. The modes of thought and language in which the early preachers of the Gospel proclaimed and interpreted these facts are historically important, but not necessarily normative today.

60 Others insist that, while Scripture gives the indispensable data for Christian belief and the life of the Church in every age, it is only through the living tradition of the Church, guided at all times by the Holy Spirit, that we can understand, interpret, and apply to the needs of the Church and the world in our day, the message which the Bible proclaims. Therefore tradition, viewed as a guide to interpretation, must be given an authority second only to that of the Bible, far superior to that of any private opinion.

61 All these views, variously modified, hold their place in the ongoing debate about divine revelation in which the Church as a whole is engaged. This debate presents a scene of tensions, even of conflicts, in both our Churches. In the light of the present world-wide turmoil in theological thinking and Biblical scholarship, this is not surprising. It is to be hoped, however, that continuing discussion, carried on in a spirit of openness and obedience towards the Scriptures themselves, will lead to the emergence in the united Church of a deeper and wider agreement on the nature of Scripture and tradition, and the relation between them, than is possible in either Church at the present time. Meanwhile, there can be no question of the exclusion of any of the views outlined above from the life of our Churches at any stage in the present scheme.

62 It should be recognized that none of these views violates the principle that what is taught as necessary to salvation must be read in, or proved by, holy Scripture. Adherence to this principle remains the common ground of the whole discussion.

63 It may be well to state explicitly that paragraphs 56–60 of the above statement were intended solely to describe the present state of opinion in our Churches. We did not and do not raise the question of the compatibility of the views there set out with the formularies, but we emphasize that there is no question of the exclusion of those who hold any of them from the life of the Church. For Stage Two, a fuller statement on the subject of Scripture and Tradition may be necessary, and in the making of such a statement both Churches will contribute their own formularies and teaching. We believe that the extent of agreement shown in the paragraphs reprinted above is sufficient for Stage One.

64 We draw attention to the latest official statement of the Church of England on this subject in the new Canon A5:

> The doctrine of the Church of England is grounded in the Holy Scriptures, and in such teachings of the ancient Fathers and Councils of the Church as are agreeable to the said Scriptures. In particular such doctrine is to be found in the Thirty-nine Articles of Religion, the Book of Common Prayer, and the Ordinal.

II. Priesthood and Ministry

Reprinted from Chapter 3 of *Towards Reconciliation*, with additional footnotes.

Background of this Statement

65 The 1963 Report prompted much discussion in both Churches of the concept of ministerial priesthood, the significance of episcopal ordination, and the Service of Reconciliation in relation to both these matters. Among the issues with which both Churches asked the Commission to deal were the interpretation of priesthood and the laying on of hands in the Service of Reconciliation. The following statement has been prepared in the light of these requests, and the discussions which preceded them.

Common Ground: Ordination and Jurisdiction

66 Our starting-point is the conviction, shared by both our Churches, that God wills his Church to have ministers of the Word and Sacraments who have been called and commissioned to their work of pastoral oversight by those to whom authority has been given in their Churches. This calling and commissioning is ordination. On the basis of this common conviction, both our Churches, in ordaining, commission men to the ministry of the Church universal, although in the nature of the case neither can confer jurisdiction (ministerial responsibility and status) beyond its own boundaries.* The Service of Reconciliation will, however, initiate an extension of jurisdiction for ministers of both Churches; hence, if for no other reason, it is right to include in it specific prayers for both ministries.

Liberty of Interpretation within Defined Limits

67 In the New Testament, ordained ministers of the Word and Sacraments are commonly called presbyters. It is asked: In what sense, if any, are they priests? To this question, which continues to provoke ecumenical discussion, Anglican answers vary, as is well known. In 1953 the Methodist Church made it a condition of the proposed conversations that 'the same liberty of interpretation of the nature of episcopacy and priesthood would be accorded to the Methodist Church as prevails in the Church of England', and the Church of England accepted this condition. What it implies is that any views which fall within the limits set by the Anglican formularies may legitimately be held by Methodists, as by Anglicans. In both our Churches, different positions regarding ministerial priesthood have been developed within the bounds set by their respective

---

* This sentence refers to the intentions of the two Churches in their ordinations.

formularies. The Commission is fully convinced that nothing in the scheme now proposed involves an adverse judgement on the theological soundness of any of these positions.

Common Ground: The Priesthood of Christ and of the Church

68   The 1963 Report sets out, and the Commission reaffirms, the common ground on this subject as follows:

(a) It is our common belief that, in the New Covenant of the Lord Jesus Christ, he alone is priest in his own right. He has offered the one perfect and final sacrifice which atones for the sins of the world, he intercedes eternally for the world, he is the one mediator between God and men; through him alone God reconciles the world to himself.

(b) By sharing in his priestly ministry, the Church corporately is a royal priesthood, a holy nation. In and under Christ it offers God's pardon and grace to the world, intercedes with God for the world, and offers itself and its worship as a living sacrifice to God.

(c) Within the corporate priesthood of the whole Church every individual believer has his own responsibility of worship, witness, and service, and his own privilege of direct personal access to God in Christ for pardon and grace.[1]

69   Different opinions are held as to the way in which the Church shares in Christ's priestly ministry, but none of these intends to call in question that the work of atoning for our sins is Christ's alone.

Ministerial Priesthood: Divergent Views

70   Discussion since 1963 has shown that the points covered in Sections (4)–(6) on pp. 23 f of the 1963 Report call for further comment. It is acknowledged that there are differences of doctrine within both Churches on the matters involved. These differences may be set out as follows:

71   Some Anglicans hold (i) that ordination within the historic episcopal succession by prayer with laying on of hands confers, in addition to grace and authority, a unique and indelible priestly character; (ii) that the ministry of presbyters who have this character is, through Christ, priestly in the sense that (a) they represent the Body of Christ in offering to God the Eucharist in which Christ's offering is made present, and (b) they represent Christ in declaring absolution to sinners, and in blessing; (iii) that non-episcopal ordinations, in that they have departed from the norm,[2] cannot be said with certainty to confer this character. These Anglicans believe their position to be supported by the Ordinal of 1662 and its Preface, and by the practice of the Church of England in confining

[1] Op. cit., p. 23.   [2] IS, p. 27.

24

to bishops and presbyters the celebration of the Eucharist and the declaring of absolution, particularly when these documents and practices are seen in the context of the Anglican appeal to Scripture and the undivided Church.*

72 Other Anglicans take a different view. They value episcopacy; they do not deny that God's call and the Church's authorization to presbyteral ministry are both for life; they affirm that a sacrifice of praise and service, responsive to the atoning sacrifice of Christ, is indeed offered at Holy Communion. But they deny that any part of the presbyter's ministry of Word or Sacrament is priestly in any sense beyond that in which the whole Church's worship is priestly. With Anglican divines of the Reformation period,[1] they understand the word 'priest' as simply a synonym for 'presbyter'. They cannot find any grounds in the theology or practice of the New Testament for regarding presbyteral ministry as in any sense sacerdotal or mediatorial, or for doubting the adequacy of non-episcopal orders, or for relating the presence and grace of Christ at the Eucharist to a representative act of offering by the minister. In support of their position they cite the teaching of the English Reformers and their successors,† and the history of Anglican relations with non-episcopal Churches and their clergy during the century after the Reformation.

73 These views of priesthood, and others lying between them, exist in the Church of England in recognized tension and recognized liberty within the unity of a common practice.‡

74 The Methodist Deed of Union (1932) states: 'Christ's ministers in the Church are stewards in the household of God and shepherds of his flock.... The Methodist Church holds the doctrine of the priesthood of

[1] e.g. Whitgift, *Works* (Parker Society), III, p. 351: 'The very word itself [sc. "priest"], as it is used in our English tongue, soundeth the word presbyter.'

---

* Some have found this paragraph ambiguous. It should, therefore, be stated that: (*a*) the statement 'ordination within the historic episcopal succession...priestly character' presupposed that ordination is the act of the Holy Spirit in response to the prayer of the Church, and that the gifts referred to are therefore conferred by God; (*b*) the term 'represent' was used in the same sense as it was used by Dr William Bright, Dr R. C. Moberly, and others, in relation to the ministerial priesthood. Cf. W. Bright, *Some Aspects of Primitive Church Life* (London, 1898), p. 58, n. 2.

† After 'successors' the words 'the history of the Ordinal' should be added.

‡ 'Recognized' here means 'recognized *de facto*'. These paragraphs describe the limits of actual divergence within our two Churches.

all believers and consequently believes that no priesthood exists which belongs exclusively to a particular order or class of men, but in the exercise of its corporate life and worship special qualifications for the discharge of special duties are required and thus the principle of representative selection is recognized.'

75   In interpreting these words, some allow that a minister may rightly be called a priest on grounds suggested by 72 above, namely that, in administering the Holy Communion and leading the worship of God's people, he is the representative of the priesthood of all believers, which is the Church. Others would not wish to use the word 'priest' of a minister, lest it imply an exclusive priesthood, though all would ascribe to the ordained ministry of the Word and Sacraments a distinctive function within the Church. Methodists agree in affirming the priesthood of all believers and in asserting that a minister is called of God to be an ambassador on behalf of Christ and a representative of the whole people of God.

76   The Methodist Conference, in its function as interpreter of Methodist doctrine, in the course of its Statement of 1960 elucidated the Deed of Union as follows:

> In the office of a minister are brought together the manifold functions of the Church's ministry, and it is his privilege to exercise them as the servant of Christ and of his fellows in the Church as a whole, as the Church under the guidance of the Spirit shall appoint him. . . . The Methodist Church is committed to the view that the ordained minister does not possess any priesthood which he does not share with the whole company of Christ's faithful people. But the doctrine of the 'priesthood of all believers' is that we share, as believers, in the priesthood of our great High Priest, Jesus Christ himself. . . . Into that priesthood of Christ we are taken up by faith, and we, in our turn, and in self-identification with him, offer ourselves in utter humility and obedience as a living sacrifice to God. We are 'priests unto God', and therefore 'take upon ourselves with joy the yoke of obedience', as we are enjoined in the Covenant Service. So the doctrine does not mean that every Christian has the right to exercise every function and administer both sacraments. For it is not an assertion of claims, but a declaration of our total obedience. A Methodist minister is a priest, in company with all Christ's faithful people; but not all priests are ministers [that is, as the context shows, 'not all members of the priesthood of all believers are ordained ministers']. Ordination is never repeated in the Methodist Church. A minister is Christ's ambassador and the representative of the whole people of God.

77   It is clear that the views of priesthood and ministry held by and within the Methodist Church fall within the limits set by the Anglican formularies, and the 'liberty of interpretation of the nature of episcopacy and priesthood', referred to in paragraph 67 above (p. 23), certainly embraces them.

The Service of Reconciliation

The bearing of what has been said upon the Service of Reconciliation is as follows:

78 Participation in the Service must not be held to imply acceptance of one rather than another of the views of priesthood mentioned above. It will imply only willingness to live in full communion with Christians who accept any of them.

79 Individual participants in the Service may be expected to bring to it diverse and opposing views of its significance for Methodist ministers, and this must be both admitted and accepted. If some see the Service as a conditional or unconditional ordination of Methodist ministers to a priesthood not hitherto exercised, others in both Churches are sure it is no such thing. If, therefore, some publicly explain it as designed to resolve doubt as to whether Methodist ministers are at present 'priests in the Church of God', others in both Churches will publicly deny the propriety of any such doubt. And if either a 'catholic' or an 'evangelical' understanding of the Service appears to be taken, even implicitly, as the norm, many at the opposite extreme will feel that their own convictions about priesthood would be compromised if they took part in it. Discussion since 1963 has emphasized this. So, if the Service is not to be intolerable for some, neither Church must officially define its significance for Methodist ministers in any other way than by saying that it will create conditions under which all Anglicans can conscientiously recognize them as 'priests in the Church of God' in whatever sense they give this phrase, so that our unfinished discussions of the presbyter's priesthood can continue within relations of full communion, and ultimately within a united Church. The common intention which the Service requires of participants is accordingly this: to commit our continuing differences to God, and on this basis to commit ourselves, with our differences, to each other.

80 From what has been said, it should be clear that this intention has a higher justification than that of expediency. It will indicate, not indifference to the theological questions that are at issue, but deep concern about them. In the judgement of the Commission, not only is a measure of disagreement about priesthood, in the words of the 1963 Report, 'not intolerable'[1] in a united Church, but a united Church is the best context for continued exploration of the differences that remain. If the intention of the Service is responsibly accepted, we may expect that, under God, our common thinking on this subject during the period of full communion, and later on in the united Church, will be theologically fruitful.

'Invariability of episcopal ordination'[2]

81 The Methodist Church is asked to accept the historic episcopate as a sign and token of the unity and continuity of the Church of Jesus Christ.

[1] Op. cit., p. 23.   [2] Ibid., p. 48, lines 19 and 25–6.

The liberty of interpretation within the limits set by Anglican formularies, referred to in paragraph 67 above (p. 23), covers differing views of episcopacy which are held within those limits in the Church of England. But the full range of this liberty of interpretation is safeguarded only if the strictest invariability of episcopal ordination is preserved. 'For, while it is possible to hold a "low" view of episcopacy within a strict invariability of practice, it becomes impossible to hold a "high" view where this invariability is broken.'[1]

82 It is for this reason that 'the strictest invariability of episcopal ordination' is basic to our proposals. Acceptance of this fact necessarily entails that, after full communion has been entered upon, all Methodist ministers in Stage One will be ordained with the laying on of hands by a bishop in the historic succession acting as chief minister in the ordination. Any variation from this practice could not but appear as a breach of a foundation-principle on which the two Churches will have come together.

83 The acceptance, however, of this rule of practice will not commit the Methodist Church as a whole, or any individual members of either Church, to the view that the historic episcopate is essential to the apostolic character of the Church, and that this character is something which non-episcopal Churches necessarily lack.

84 Nor will the acceptance of this rule imply assent to the view (erroneously thought to be current in the Church of England) that the grace of God, freely offered to men in Jesus Christ, flows into the Church only through the channel of the historic episcopate; still less, that membership of an episcopally ordered Church is a necessary condition of salvation, additional to faith in Christ. No such views are required, nor will be required, of any members of either Church.

85 Rather, the acceptance of the historic episcopate and of the 'strictest invariability of episcopal ordination' will indicate, on the one hand, an unwillingness in either Church to attempt to bring the two Churches together in a way that would create divisions between Anglicans; and, on the other, a desire on the Methodist side to share as fully as possible, though with liberty of interpretation, in a form of ministry which has been inherited from the Christian past and offers the best hope of unity throughout the world.

The Laying on of Hands

86 In the New Testament the laying on of hands appears in a number of different connections. It is associated with healing in the ministry of Jesus and the Apostles (Mark 5. 23; 6. 5; Acts 28. 8). It is associated with ordination in 1 Timothy 4. 14; see also Acts 6. 6, 1 Timothy 5. 22, and

[1] Ibid., p. 48.

2 Timothy 1. 6, where ordination may be referred to. It is associated with the appointment to a further mission of those already ordained (Acts 13. 3). It is associated with the coming of the Holy Spirit (Acts 8. 17; 19. 6). It is referred to, apparently in connection with Baptism, in Hebrews 6. 2. There is a similar variety of associations in the usage of the Church throughout its history. In the practice of the Church of England, the rite is found in various contexts, including not only such once-for-all occasions as confirmation and ordination, but also others where repetition is possible, such as acts of blessing and healing. In current Methodist practice the laying on of hands is used in the ordination of ministers and deaconesses, the commissioning of missionaries, both ministerial and lay, and on occasion in the Service of Public Reception of full members.

87   In many New Testament contexts where it appears, the laying on of hands symbolizes the purpose of sharing with another some function, gift, benefit, or responsibility, which one has oneself received from God, and which God now wills to be passed on. It also expresses the self-identification and solidarity of one person, or group of persons, with another.

88   In the life of the Church the rite is regularly accompanied by prayer, which declares what it is that is being shared with, and desired for, the person on whom hands are laid. This prayer is thus of the essence of the action, in which the laying on of hands itself has the significance of an outward and visible sign of the application of the prayer to a particular individual. In the Service of Reconciliation, therefore, the key to understanding the mutual laying on of hands (which is performed in silence) must be sought in the prayers which surround it.

89   That the laying on of the bishop's hands will convey ordination to the priesthood to those who have not previously received it is undoubtedly one possible interpretation of the prayer preceding this act in the Service. It is clear that many could not take part in the Service were they denied liberty so to interpret it, just as many could not take part were they required so to interpret it. But what is done at this point has a significance which can and should command the assent of all. The laying on of hands is reciprocal: as episcopal hands are laid on Methodist ministers, so the hands of Methodist ministers are laid on Anglican bishops and priests. And in each case the explicit burden of the preceding prayer is that the Spirit may bestow on those on whom hands are laid such gifts as they need in order to fulfil their ministry in each other's Churches. The rite thus visibly declares that the two ministries now being reconciled, and the Churches which they represent, are praying that each ministry may be enabled to share with the other the gifts of the Spirit which it has received in its separation, and that the two ministries may be fully identified with each other in the wider mission which they are about to undertake together.

III. The Doctrine of Holy Communion :
Sacrificial Aspects
Reprinted from Chapter 4 of *Towards Reconciliation*

Introduction

90 'If we are to achieve full communion with each other, we must be assured that there is sufficient harmony in our sacramental doctrine and practice to make common worship at the Lord's Table a practical and unifying reality.'[1] In order to give assurance on this point, the Report first listed the places where the sacramental teaching of the Church of England is found[2] and then printed a 'fairly representative' modern Methodist statement on both sacraments, which it hoped that Anglicans would receive 'as indicating that there is sufficient doctrinal basis for closer relations in the sacramental life of the two Churches'.[3] The authors of the Dissentient View feared that the references to Eucharistic sacrifice would cause disquiet through being too unguarded, and called for closer definition, both positive and negative.[4] The 1965 Methodist Conference asked the Joint Commission to clarify 'the sacrificial aspects of Holy Communion'. The following paragraphs have been written in the light of these requests.

Common Ground

91 Within both our Churches there are long-standing differences of opinion about the sacrificial aspects of the Holy Communion. Discussion of them has been hampered and obscured by deep-seated fears, on the one side of 'the Mass', and on the other side of the view of the sacrament as 'a bare memorial', which is often, though dubiously, ascribed to Zwingli. The presence of these fears has tended to conceal the amount of common ground which all parties to the discussion share. It is significant that the present Methodist Book of Offices contains the Holy Communion Service of the 1662 Prayer Book, almost unchanged. Some of the main agreements within and between our two Churches are:

92 It is agreed that both the sacraments of the gospel are of divine appointment and perpetual obligation.

93 It is agreed that the Holy Communion is a sign, and an occasion, and a means, of the saving presence of Jesus Christ with his faithful people, whereby he bestows on them the benefits of his one, perfect, and sufficient sacrifice and so unites them more closely to himself and in himself to each other.

---

[1] *Report*, p. 28.
[2] Articles XXV–XXXI, and the Prayer Book services and catechism.
[3] *Report*, p. 29.   [4] Ibid., p. 61.

94 It is agreed that at the Holy Communion we respond to God's redeeming love by offering him our praise and thanksgiving in union with the whole Church in heaven and on earth. In thanksgiving for our redemption we offer to God our gifts of money, and ourselves to be his servants. All these offerings, together with our corporate recollection of the sacrifice of Christ, and our consuming of bread and wine in remembrance of him, make up 'our bounden duty and service' in the rite as a whole.

95 It is agreed that we make these responsive offerings through Christ's mediation, in which we trust; on the basis of his sacrifice made once for all, which we invoke; and in the strength of his Spirit, on whom we rely. It is as those who are in Christ that the people of God offer themselves to him at the Lord's Supper. As repentant and believing sinners, accepted and renewed in him, they present themselves to be wholly identified with Christ in his death, so that his risen life may appear in them ever more fully, 'until he come'.

96 It is agreed that the Eucharist is not in any sense a repeating, or augmenting, or supplementing, of the complete and perfect atonement wrought by Jesus Christ on the cross. 'Any view of the Eucharist that implies that the work of Christ was "unfinished" in the sense that we can add to it by anything we do, or that it needs to be done again, must be repudiated as unscriptural.'[1]

97 These agreements, in the judgement of the Commission, form 'sufficient doctrinal basis for closer relations in the sacramental life of the two Churches'.

Varieties of Conviction

98 Many in both our Churches would not want to go beyond the beliefs which form the common ground between them. It is enough for them to offer devotion to their risen Lord, who suffered, rose, and ascended for their salvation, and is present at his Table to give himself to all who will receive him. Others would express their belief that in this sacrament Christ bestows the benefits of his atoning sacrifice by saying that he does this in answer to our pleading of its efficacy and our presentation of it anew to the Father. This is the way in which they understand his command, 'Do this in remembrance of me'. The act of *anamnesis*, translated 'remembrance', is, on this view, an act by which we bring to remembrance before God what Christ has done for us. For those who hold this view, this act of remembrance is closely related to the consecration of the bread and wine to be the Body and Blood of the Lord. Many Methodists and Anglicans, however, cannot find Biblical warrant for this understanding of 'remembrance' in terms of presentation anew, and take Christ's command

[1] *Report*, p. 32.

rather to mean that, as we receive the sacramental bread and wine, all that Christ did for us, and all that he eternally does for us in the heavenly places, is effectively applied to our benefit in the Eucharistic mystery. Our 'remembrance of him' thus becomes dynamic and efficacious for our sanctification through the working of the Holy Spirit.

99 The Eucharistic hymns of the Wesleys powerfully express belief in the eternal significance of the sacrifice of Christ, 'As now for guilty sinners slain',[1] though beyond this the exact meaning of their sacrificial imagery is still under discussion by scholars. These hymns have never been among the official formularies of Methodist doctrine, but they are very highly valued by many in both our Churches.

100 These and similar varieties of belief have never led to the breakdown of Eucharistic fellowship within either of our Churches, and do not form a barrier to full communion between the two Churches in the future.

FURTHER COMMENTS

101 Paragraphs 90–100 do not repudiate a view held in both Churches and referred to in the fifth and final point of the Statement on Holy Communion printed on pp. 31–3 of the 1963 Report, which reads as follows: 'The sacrament of Holy Communion is a sacrifice. Any view of the Eucharist that implies that the work of Christ was "unfinished" in the sense that we can add to it by anything we do, or that it needs to be done again, must be repudiated as unscriptural. The background of the Eucharist is the sacrifice of Christ, and Christ alone, on the Cross. It is that we represent, and re-present and renew by our remembrance and communion.'

These paragraphs do not purport to give a full account of eucharistic theology in either of our Churches, and are not meant to be read in isolation. We now append to them, therefore, a recapitulation of the first four points of the 1963 statement, as a reminder of the wider context within which our differences about eucharistic sacrifice are set. It should be recalled that the 1963 statement was a Methodist statement, described as 'fairly representative' of Methodist teaching.

102 Holy Communion is _an act of Jesus Christ_. 'In Holy Communion what signifies primarily is not what the Church does but what Christ has done, is doing and waiting to do. He is _hospes atque epulum_ (host and food)—Zwingli's phrase. Christ himself presides and gives himself to be the life of his people.'

[1] Methodist Hymn Book, No. 771.

103 Holy Communion is *an act of remembrance*, 'by which, through the renewal of the corporate memory of the Church by the Holy Spirit, the great "salvation" events culminating in the Cross are re-enacted. This act of corporate recollection embraces not only the past but the future and what lies beyond history in the consummation of the kingdom of God.'

104 Holy Communion is *a means of fellowship with Christ*. 'The act of remembrance leads to communion. He who is remembered is the living Christ offering to us the bread that is the life of God himself, the life that came through death. By feeding upon him, we become his body. "This is my body." It is the body offered that he gives to us and as we receive it, we become his body through which his life, not our own, pulsates. Holy Communion is a sacrament of the Real Presence.'

105 [While aware of the history of controversy that lies behind the phrase 'Real Presence', we would endorse the following assertions, on which, we are told, there was 'a very large measure of agreement' in the recently concluded Anglican–Presbyterian conversations: 'In the Sacrament Christ himself acts and is present with his people. It is not necessary, and perhaps not possible, to give an exact account of the manner of this presence. This presence is to be related not only to the elements of bread and wine but also to the whole action of minister and people together. The people's faith does not create the presence but simply acknowledges it' (*The Anglican–Presbyterian Conversations* (1966), p. 28).]

106 Holy Communion is *a manifesting of union with other Christians*. 'Our communion with Christ in this sacrament means that we are united to each other. We are sinners in need of a common saviour. We are branches of the same vine. We appear at the Holy Table before the face of the one Father. Further, the Church militant and the Church triumphant are present at the Eucharist. "One family we dwell in him." As members of the same family we share the same loaf and become hungry for that upon which we feed.'

107 We reaffirm the claim of the 1963 Report, made in the light of these common affirmations, that 'in the interpretation of Holy Communion as well as Baptism there is, amid divisive issues that must not be shirked, an impressive measure of agreement between us' (p. 31).

4 Why Two Stages?

The Legacy of Separation

108   It may be asked why, if union is the goal, a first stage of full communion without union should be thought necessary. The answer is that nothing else is practicable. During the time of their separation, which has now lasted for a century and three-quarters, the Church of England and the Methodist Church have lived in isolation from one another. During this period there have been many developments in Anglican thought, worship, and practice. The Methodist Church has not by any means forsaken either the doctrines or the way of life and worship which it inherited from the Church of England, but it too has produced and matured its own formulations of its teaching and its own traditions and methods of devotion and the ordering of church life. Most members of both Churches have grown up in ignorance of each other's ways. Differences of approach to worship and order often turn out on close and friendly examination to be superficial and insignificant, but meanwhile they loom large in the minds of many clergy, ministers, and lay people. So it would not be possible for the two Churches to become effectively one, in full fellowship together, through a single act of unification in the near future. Time for growth in mutual understanding is needed before a union which involves the setting up of a single administrative unit and system of government can be successfully attempted. The imposing of organizational union before the members of our two Churches were fully prepared for it would bring bewilderment and bitterness in plenty, and this cannot be the right way to proceed.

Complicating Factors

109   Also, the complex and distinctive relationship of the Church of England to the State presents difficulties to Methodists in its present form, and this fact in itself makes an immediate organic union impracticable from the Methodist standpoint. The form of the Establishment is, indeed, under review, but changes are likely to take some years to be accepted and carried out.

110   Moreover, the Church of England's position as the nodal point of the Anglican Communion is bound to be substantially affected by

its union with what is now a non-episcopal Church, and this matter will need to be carefully discussed over a number of years with the other Churches involved, before actual union is attempted. Similarly, it is realized that the union of the Methodist Church in this country with the Church of England will have far-reaching implications for the world-wide family of Methodist Churches, in the councils of which British Methodism holds an honoured and historic place.

The Way Forward

111 All these difficulties are capable of resolution within a reasonable time. But the need for closer unity now is urgent and compelling. This is why the 1963 Report proposed that union should be achieved in two stages: the first stage to be inaugurated by the entering of the two Churches into full communion with each other, and the taking of episcopacy into the Methodist system; the second, following as soon as possible, to take the form of visible, organic union into one Church. Thus the best possible conditions for the growth of mutual knowledge, understanding, and trust will be created, inasmuch as the Churches will from the start be bound together by sacramental fellowship in the Body and Blood of Christ.

Meanwhile, time will allow for working out the long-term problems of achieving a united Church. This is why the 1958 Interim Statement, after speaking of the proposals for the unification of the ministries in North India and Ceylon, and of the lessons which can be learned from them, commends a two-stage scheme for England in these words: 'This method of action would at once remove the worst sin and scandal of disunity, and would open the door to that growing together in and through which we may expect to be led by the Holy Spirit to see how to take each successive step, until we reach that unity, visible and invisible, which is according to God's will' (*IS*, p. 44).

112 This does not mean that intercommunion is being used merely as a means to the end of organic union, but rather that the stage of full communion is an integral part of the process towards it, and a foretaste of what is at the heart of the union that is to be.

5 Methodist Bishops

Historic Episcopacy

113　It is implicit in the present negotiations for Anglican–Methodist union that the Methodist Church should become an episcopal Church at Stage One, and that the united Church of the future should be episcopal. The episcopacy which the Methodist Church is invited to 'take into its system' is 'historic' episcopacy, exercised through men consecrated in the historic episcopate. The majority of Christians throughout the world live within communions which have this historic episcopate, though that is not in itself a compelling reason why the Methodist Church should adopt it. However, in the present scheme further considerations operate.

114　All union schemes between Churches with the historic episcopate and other Churches have provided for the retention of the historic episcopate in the united Church. The Methodist Church of Great Britain has readily agreed to this for her daughter Churches involved in union schemes in South India, North India, Nigeria, Ghana, and Ceylon, and there is no instance in which she has refused to agree to it. What is envisaged in the present scheme is a domestic application of this same principle. The present question is how Methodists at home are to receive for themselves what they have approved for Methodists overseas. But before we go on to this question, it is worth while considering the nature of the historic episcopate both as Anglicans now see it and as Methodists and Anglicans will, we hope, see it in the future. Such consideration will, perhaps, show to Methodists who have hesitations about accepting historic episcopacy that their objections are to certain theories of it to which many Anglicans also object, and not to historic episcopacy in itself.

115　What is meant by 'the historic episcopate' was discussed in the 1958 Interim Statement, pp. 20–7. It is summed up in two sentences from the 1930 Lambeth Conference statement: 'When we speak of the historic episcopate, we mean the episcopate as it emerged in the clear light of history from the time when definite evidence begins to be available.... What we uphold is the episcopate, maintained in successive generations by continuity of succession and consecration,

36

as it has been throughout the history of the Church from the earliest times, and discharging those functions which from the earliest times it has discharged.'

116 What those functions are was outlined in the 1938 Report, *Doctrine in the Church of England*. These were quoted *in extenso* both in the 1958 Interim Statement (pp. 25 and 26) and in the 1963 Report (pp. 24 and 25). The whole section reads:

> The argument for Episcopacy derives its strength from the convergence of many considerations. We may state these in summary form; but the very nature of the office depends upon the union of all these elements.
>
> (i) The episcopate symbolizes and secures in an abiding form the apostolic mission and authority within the Church; historically the episcopate became the organ of this mission and authority.
>
> (ii) In early times the continuous successions of bishops in tenure of the various sees were valued because they secured the purity of apostolic teaching as against, for example, the danger of the introduction of novel and erroneous teaching by means of writings or secret traditions falsely ascribed to apostolic authors. No doubt the need for this safeguard became less urgent when authoritative formulations of doctrine were drawn up and the canon of scripture finally fixed. But it has remained a function of the episcopate to guard the Church against erroneous teaching.
>
> (iii) The bishop in his official capacity represents the whole Church in and to his diocese, and his diocese in and to the councils of the Church. He is thus a living representative of the unity and universality of the Church.
>
> (iv) The bishop in his diocese represents the Good Shepherd; the idea of pastoral care is inherent in his office. Both clergy and laity look to him as chief pastor, and he represents in a special degree the paternal quality of pastoral care.
>
> (v) Inasmuch as the unity of the Church is in part secured by an orderly method of making new ministers and the bishop is the proper organ of unity and universality, he is the appropriate agent for carrying on through ordination the authority of the apostolic mission of the Church.

117 These Five Points constitute the essential 'norm' from which most Anglicans believe they 'ought not to and cannot depart'. They are secured in all the other union schemes involving Anglicans to which British Methodism has agreed. The Anglican Communion has never officially endorsed any one particular theory of the origin of the historic episcopate, its exact relation to the apostolate, and the sense in which it should be thought of as God-given, and in fact tolerates a wide variety of views on these points. The same liberty (see para. 67)

will be extended to Methodists. Methodists could not, nor would Anglicans expect them to, accept any interpretation which would regard episcopal ordination as necessary for a Christian body to be accepted as part of the Church, or episcopal succession as an exclusive channel of the grace of God. But the Methodist acceptance of episcopacy is not negative or grudging. The 1958 Interim Statement (pp. 35 and 36) saw it as a precious gift in the acceptance of which God might be asking Methodism to find a confirmation and enrichment of its own inheritance. Methodists recognize that 'the possession of this "Continuing Commission" not only constitutes a visible and significant bond between the Churches of Christendom, but links the present with the life of the primitive Church in a fellowship which gathers to itself the treasures of the ages'.

118 The 1963 Report declared that in accepting the historic episcopate: '[Methodists] are conscious that they are moving throughout not in the context of mere name or jurisdiction but in that of apostolicity, with all that that means for the doctrine of God and his Church' (p. 25).

119 Yet this acceptance looks to the future even more than to the past. 'The Church of England is inviting Methodism, not to adopt a third- or fourth-century model of episcopacy any more than an eighteenth-century English model, but to join in a search for what episcopacy might become for us and our children' (IS, p. 18). The shape of the future episcopacy in the united Church cannot be known until our Churches have grown so effectively together that they can combine the strength of Anglican constitutional episcopacy as it has developed in the twentieth century with the vitality of the diversified *episcopé* (pastoral care and oversight) which at present is exercised in Methodism by the Conference, the Chairmen, and the Circuit Superintendents, and can see what fresh adaptations of this dual heritage are called for to meet the needs of our times.

120 But it should be said at once that Methodist bishops need not and must not be confined to the performance of a round of administrative duties. The Methodist people would be grievously disappointed if their bishops did not also undertake tasks of imaginative and creative leadership in thought and action. Experiments and enterprises in mission and in the training of Christians, some already begun under present leadership, are looking for the yet stronger lead that a truly pastoral episcopate, working together with its Anglican counterpart, will be able to give. Methodist bishops will vindicate their office by evangelistic and pastoral leadership. Above all, a Methodist bishop will

be valued as a father-in-God to the ministers in his care. This pastoral office, essential to the well-being both of the ministers themselves and of the congregations entrusted to them, is already carried out in good measure by the Chairmen of Districts; it is very desirable that bishops in the Methodist Church should be left sufficiently free from routine administration to be able to maintain and develop what has been thus begun, as well as to strike out new lines of approach to evangelism and the service of the community.

The Functions of Methodist Bishops

121   The nature of episcopacy, as we understand it, may be gathered from the Preface to the Ordinal and Form of Consecration in Part 1 of this Report. The following summary shows how these functions might be exercised in Methodism during Stage One.

122   All episcopacy belongs to Christ, the Good Shepherd, and the bishop's commission by Christ expressly assigns him to be the chief pastor of the ministers and the people in his charge. As father-in-God to both he is called to feed the flock of Christ in tender concern for their well-being, not as a lord and master, but as a servant of the servants of Christ.

123   Both as pastor and guardian the bishop must, whenever necessary, within the framework of the Methodist Constitution, see that discipline is exercised within the fellowship of the Church, and that in all such matters every proper step is taken to heal, forgive, restore, or, when all else fails, to rebuke, reprimand, or exclude. Discipline includes not only the proper operation of church courts, and the pastoral care of those who have erred, but the oversight of teaching and preaching and the supervision of public worship.

124   Continuity with the historic episcopate will both initially and thereafter be effectively maintained, it being understood that no one particular interpretation of the historic episcopate as accepted by the Methodist Church is thereby implied, or shall be demanded from any minister or member of it.

125   Bishops shall officiate in the ordination of all Methodist ministers and in the consecration of bishops.

126   Consecration to the episcopate, like ordination to the ministry, shall be for life. It will be possible, however, for a bishop to return to circuit work, while retaining the order and title of bishop.

39

The Appointment of Bishops in Methodism

127 The appointment of Methodist bishops should be governed by the above principles, but the method of appointment is a matter to be decided by the Methodist Church itself. The tradition of the Connexional system requires that the appointing body must be the Methodist Conference. Here we would indicate some of the factors that need to be considered by the Conference, and venture some suggestions, simply to show the range of questions involved.

128 Two provisions have to be made: (a) the selection and appointment of the first Methodist bishops who will be consecrated by bishops of the Anglican Communion and, if desired, by other bishops in the historic episcopate, and (b) the procedure for the election of subsequent bishops within Methodism to fill vacancies and new appointments.

129 Adhering to the principle that there must be the least possible disturbance of the Methodist Constitution, there would seem to be a strong case for appointing as bishops those ministers whose present work most embodies the functions of *episcopē*. The President during his year of office represents the Church and is the guardian of its discipline. He is father-in-God to the whole Church and pastor of pastors. Between Conferences much of the authority of the Church rests in him and he has wide powers, both legal and ecclesiastical. He is also the chief ordaining officer of the Church. As long as Methodism continues as a separate body, it is difficult to conceive its appointing other men as bishops and not the President.

130 Ex-Presidents frequently deputize for the President and share with him the conduct of ordination. The number involved is not great. At present there are nine ex-Presidents in active work. It will be for the Conference to decide how many, if any, ex-Presidents should be consecrated. These suggestions were made in the 1963 Report, p. 54: 'It would seem desirable, therefore, that any minister on his appointment as President of the Conference should, if he is not already a bishop, be consecrated, and the duties now devolving upon the President and upon the ex-Presidents in relation to ordination and other matters should continue to be discharged by them.'

131 Chairmen of Districts exercise many of the powers and functions of the diocesan bishop. The Chairmen are chief pastors to both the ministry and the Methodist people; they exercise discipline and oversight, they preside at all Synod meetings (save when the Presi-

dent is present); they have oversight of the circuits in their districts. They are charged with the leadership of the district, especially in its mission to evangelize. The fact that they have this territorial oversight, and already discharge much of the episcopal office, would seem to point to them as men whom Methodism would also select as its bishops.

132 The main difference is that Chairmen do not ordain. This is done at Conference, for Methodist ministers belong to the Connexion, not to districts. This principle is enshrined in the present practice of ordination at Conference by the President and ex-Presidents with presbyters assisting in the laying on of hands. But the Chairman as bishop could share with the President in the ordination of those ordinands sent forward by his own district.

133 There are thirty-four districts in British Methodism of which twenty-six in England, one in Scotland, and one in Wales have 'separated'[1] Chairmen. The three island districts and the three Welsh-speaking districts have too small a membership to support separated Chairmen. The present districts with separated Chairmen contain an average of about 24,000 members. It would be for Conference to decide whether all or some of the Chairmen should be appointed bishops, and how this situation should be met in Wales and Scotland.

134 If the President-Designate were not already a bishop, his consecration could take place either as part of his induction or in a special service, as Conference may decide.

135 If the present plan of reconciliation is accepted, then Conference would have to give immediate attention to the election of its first bishops and to the machinery for future elections. We suggest that if the proposals are adopted, the Conference of 1969 should appoint either the General Purposes and Policy Committee, or some special committee, to make such nominations and devise such machinery, and to report to the Conference of 1970, to which the reports from the Synods on the scheme as a whole will come. This would enable the Church to proceed directly to the act of reconciliation and the consecration of the first Methodist bishops during the year following.

136 Whatever system Conference adopts for the subsequent election of bishops, it must be ensured that as long as Methodism remains a

[1] 'Separated', i.e. without local pastoral charge. The Chairman is separated from the ordinary circuit ministry in order to devote his full time to the life and work of the district.

Connexion the final election must be by Conference itself, as is now the case with the appointment of Chairmen. The office of bishop is not just a district matter, but belongs to the whole Church. Hence the need for the final judgement to remain with Conference, though the Synod concerned should be represented fully and given the most complete liberty to express its mind.

Relations with the Anglican Episcopate

137 From the beginning of the two parallel Churches it would be in every way desirable that at least once a year Methodist and Anglican bishops should meet for fellowship, consultation, and the sharing of common concerns.

138 There are many ways in which the bishops of each Church can help one another, both locally and nationally. Urgent problems clamour for joint planning and action not only in new areas and towns, but in the areas of industrial blight and in the depopulated countryside. As the two Churches grow closer together new opportunities for co-operation will appear, the whole purpose of which is to make more effective in our land the work and witness of the two Churches.

139 From this joint experience the bishops will be able to advise those who during Stage One will be charged with formulating the proposals for the shape of the episcopate in the united Church. The concept of episcopacy is not static and is at present developing rapidly in episcopal Churches throughout the world. Methodist experience of *episcopē* within the Connexional system will contribute significantly to that new thinking. These present proposals, however, relate only to Methodist bishops in the transitional period of Stage One.

6 One Ordinal for Both Churches

The Importance of the Ordinal

140   The majority of worshippers in both our Churches may never have attended an Ordination, and may never attend one. Yet the ordination procedure is of crucial importance in the life of any Church. In the first place, ministers are key people, and the whole direction of their ministry will be controlled by the commission given them when they are ordained. Many Anglican clergy regularly re-read the Prayer Book service for the Ordering of Priests, to remind themselves what they are called to be; many Methodist ministers look back to their own Ordination service for the same purpose. Also, the way a Church ordains its candidates is a decisive pointer to what it believes about the ministry itself. The Anglican Ordinal is regularly appealed to in debate as one of the authorized formularies establishing the doctrine of the Church of England, and in 1960 the Methodist Conference declared: 'The Ordination Service, of course, has much light to throw on the teaching of the Methodist Church on this subject' (i.e. the Church and its ministry).[1]

The Need for a Common Ordinal

141   Rightly, therefore, did the 1963 Report declare it to be desirable that before Stage One begins 'the Church of England and the Methodist Church should jointly revise their respective ordinals, so that by the use of a service of ordination which is common to both Churches unity may be furthered, and ground for suspicion and criticism removed' (p. 37). The reference to removing suspicion reminds us of the fact that some in both Churches have affirmed that the understanding of the Christian ministry maintained by the other is basically different from that of their own Church. The reference to furthering unity reminds us that common ideals for the ministry, which a common Ordinal would express, will naturally become a growing-point of fellowship, inasmuch as they will tend to shape the whole of our thinking about the Church's organized life, and to ensure that henceforth in both Churches it will proceed along similar lines.

[1]   *MBM*, p. 7, from the statement on Ordination.

43

142 Further reasons may be given for thinking it appropriate to secure a common Ordinal at the outset of Stage One. First, the doctrine of the ministry is a disputed issue outside our two Churches no less than within them, and it is desirable to show the rest of Christendom straight away, and as clearly as possible, what common view of this doctrine our Churches maintain. Then it is much to be hoped that both Anglican and Methodist bishops will from the start of Stage One normally share in every consecration that takes place in either Church, to make it plain that unity between the two at ministerial level is a living and growing reality, and this makes the use of a common Ordinal doubly fitting. Moreover, the Methodist Church will have to alter its Ordinal at the beginning of Stage One in any case, since it will henceforth be ordaining within the framework, not of a single presbyteral order, but of a threefold ministry. These facts together provide ample warrant for the venture of producing the new draft Ordinal which, with its text revised and its Preface rewritten in the light of comments on the original draft (*TR*, pp. 51–75), has now been issued as Part I of this Report.

The Doctrine of the Ordinal[1]

143 The doctrine of the ministry which the Ordination Services embody, and which the two Churches, if they accept the services, will henceforth be pledged unitedly to uphold, is set forth with care in the Preface. Here the positive emphases which characterized the thinking of both Churches on this subject while they were separate are brought together. Associated especially with Anglicanism is a stress on the historical continuity of the threefold ministry from the early days of Christianity, its significance as a focal point in the visible unity of God's people, and the divine authority with which ordained ministers act. Associated especially with Methodism is an insistence that the ordained ministry fulfils a specific representative function within the corporate priesthood of the whole people of God. The concept of ordination as an act of God the Holy Spirit answering the prayers of the Church—a New Testament concept, reflected in the earliest ordination procedures of which we know and held with equal conviction by both our Churches—is stated precisely. So also is the fundamental point that the meaning of the Church's action in calling and sending ministers must be explained in terms of the apostolic vocation, mission, and commission, which the Church itself, in and under Christ, has received from its Lord. The whole statement calls for careful study. For convenience, and because of its importance, we reproduce it as an appendix to this chapter.

[1] Cf. paragraph 47 above.

144 One point in the text of the Ordinal needs special mention, namely, the reversion from the Anglican 'priest' and Methodist 'minister' to the older title of 'presbyter' for the second order of the historic ministry. Comparison of the new Ordinal with its predecessors will show that the change of name does not involve any change of doctrine at this point for either Church, and it is not expected nor desired that 'priest' and 'minister' should vanish from our ordinary speech. We realize that each of these words has for many people long and deeply treasured associations. But we believe that, as well as being a non-controversial word, which cannot be said of 'priest', 'presbyter' is actually more catholic, more correct, and clearer. It is more catholic because, unlike 'priest', it is a recognized name throughout the whole of Christendom for this order of ministry. It is more correct, because it is the standard New Testament name for a member of this order. It is clearer, because the use of 'priest' for one of the three orders is confusing when some Christians think of ministerial priesthood as held in common by both presbyters and bishops, and others prefer to confine the term 'priesthood' to the priesthood which is shared by all Christian believers. These two traditions will be in direct dialogue as our Churches come together, and it would be undesirable to appear to prejudice the issues by requiring Methodists to conform to Anglican usage. We believe that mature consideration will commend the course that we have taken.

The 1963 Report said, in relation to the acceptance of episcopacy by the Methodist Church: 'Assurance will be required that the specific functions of a priest within the Church of God would be safeguarded in practice, by confining the celebration of the Eucharist to bishops and priests, and by acknowledging as part of the priestly and ministerial office the declaring the absolution and remission of their sins to penitent sinners.' The new Ordinal meets the second of these points by stating explicitly that among the duties of a presbyter is to absolve the penitent in Christ's Name. It also, in both the ordination of presbyters and the consecration of bishops, speaks of the celebration of the Eucharist as among the functions of these offices, and it should be understood as part of the agreement in the coming together of the two Churches that the celebration of the Eucharist will be confined in both to bishops and presbyters, save for the temporary exception in the Methodist Church mentioned in Chapter 9, paragraphs 179–82 below.

APPENDIX:
PART OF THE PREFACE TO THE
DRAFT ORDINAL[1]

Reprinted from Part I (The Ordinal) of this Report

PREFACE

THE MINISTRY IN THE CHURCH

145 God the Father sent his Son Jesus Christ into the world to reconcile men to himself and to gather together in one flock the company of the redeemed which is the Church of God. At Pentecost the Holy Spirit was sent upon the Church to inspire and to sanctify. The Church herself, in the power of the Holy Spirit, is sent by her Lord to preach the Gospel to the ends of the earth, to bring men to the knowledge of him so that being incorporated into his body they may there grow to the measure of the stature of the fullness of Christ.

146 The risen and ascended Lord has made his people 'kings and priests unto God and his Father' (Rev. 1. 6). All the baptized are members of his Body, a royal priesthood consecrated to God's service. They exercise their priesthood by prayer and thanksgiving, joining together in the celebration of the Lord's Supper, and by their witness of life and word, in all of which they show forth the Gospel of salvation. Christ the Lord is prophet, priest, and king, and the Church, the New Israel, reflects this triple office in her witness, worship, and common life. The New Israel, incorporated in Christ, is called to show forth his love towards mankind by proclaiming God to the world, by serving human need in all its forms, and by leading the world to worship and serve God.

147 The New Testament shows the Church on the Day of Pentecost as a body of believers having within it, as its recognized focus of unity and organ of authority, the Apostolate, which the Lord himself instituted. As the Report *Doctrine in the Church of England* says: 'There was not first an Apostolate which gathered a body of believers about itself; nor was there a completely structureless collection of believers which gave authority to the Apostles to speak and act on its behalf. To suppose that the organization of the Church must have begun in one or other of these ways is to misconceive the situation. From the first there was the fellowship of believers finding its unity in the Twelve. Thus the New Testament bears witness to the principle of a distinctive Ministry, as an original element, but not the sole constitutive element, in the life of the Church.' So also the *Statement on the Nature of the Church according to the teaching of the Methodists* says: 'In the New Testament the ministry of the Word and Sacraments is a divine gift to the Church, and was in those early days an integral

[1] *Anglican–Methodist Unity*, Part I, *The Ordinal*, pp. 11–13.

46

part of its organic life. It was a ministry within the Church, exercising in the name and by the authority of the Lord, who is the Head of the Church, powers and functions which are inherent in the Church.'

148   The royal priesthood which the whole Church has received from Christ her Lord, and in which each member of his Body shares, is exercised by the faithful in different ways. The distinctive Ministry is a special form of this participation. It is in this way that the priesthood of bishop and presbyter should be understood.

149   The Ministry is thus a divinely appointed organ which acts in relation to the whole Body in the name of Christ and which represents the priestly service of the whole Body in its common worship. Ministers are, as the Methodist *Statement on Ordination* says, both Christ's ambassadors and the representatives of the whole people of God.

ORDINATION AND THE ORDINAL

150   Ordination is a solemn act by which one who is acknowledged to have received God's call is brought into a particular Order of Ministry within the Church. Central to it is the action of the Holy Spirit in bestowing upon the person being ordained that which makes him a minister. The words of the Ordination Prayer indicate what that is in respect of each Order. As Hooker says: 'The power and authority delivered with these words is itself charisma, a gracious donation which the Spirit of God doth bestow.' Those who voice the prayer are themselves already ministers with authority to ordain, and they accompany it by laying their hands on those who are being ordained. Both Churches present their candidates in the belief that the Holy Spirit will act in response to this prayer. Thus, for both, prayer with the laying on of hands is the outward sign whereby the ordinand receives the gift of the Spirit making him a minister. Both Churches regard ordination as for life, and in neither is ordination to any particular Order ever repeated.

151   The commission given by Christ to the apostles has been perpetuated in the Church, and it is the desire of the Church of England and the Methodist Church, in following God's call to unity, faithfully to preserve and transmit this commission in their ordinations. The two Churches have provided in this Ordinal forms by which the historic Ministry may be continued among them and which they agree to use when they ordain men to any of the three Orders of Bishop, Presbyter, and Deacon.

152   The form of ordination in each case follows the scriptural pattern of acceptance by the people and prayer with the laying on of hands. In each, therefore, will be found the presentation of candidates to the Presiding Bishop, which is the last step in the process of choice by the Church, and prayer for that gift of the Holy Spirit which is needed for

the work of the Order to which the person is being ordained, together with the laying on of hands by the Presiding Bishop. At least two other bishops will join in the laying on of hands at the Consecration of Bishops, and not fewer than three presbyters at the Ordination of Presbyters. The titles used for each of the three Orders are found in Scripture and were those used in the ordination rites of the undivided Church; thus they indicate the continuity of each Order with the historic Ministry. The nature of each Order is indicated more fully by the functions which it performs in the Church, the more important of which are specified in each case in the Examination and the Ordination Prayer.

7 Future Relations with Other Churches

Present Relationship

153 Both the Church of England and the Methodist Church belong to world-wide communions, and neither wishes by coming together with the other to jeopardize the relations of full communion and spiritual fellowship which each of them now enjoys with the other members of its own ecclesiastical family, many of them autonomous. This would be to promote one kind of unity at the expense of another, and so to set back rather than to further the total unity of Christendom, towards which Anglican–Methodist unity is meant to be a step.

154 Also, each Church stands in relations of full communion with other Churches not of its own family. The Bonn Agreement of 1931 established such relations between the Church of England and the Churches of the Union of Utrecht (the Old Catholics), and similar agreements have been made between the Church of England and three other Churches with an episcopate in the historic line of succession—the Spanish Reformed Episcopal Church, the Philippine Independent Church, and the Lusitanian Church. In addition, the Church of England stands in relations of limited intercommunion which have been explicitly negotiated with the Churches of Sweden, Finland, and the Church of South India, whose episcopates are in the historic succession, and with the Churches of Norway, Iceland, Denmark, Latvia, and Estonia, whose episcopates are not. The Methodist Church has not entered into negotiated agreements with other Churches in this way, but it understands itself to be in full communion with other Free Churches in Britain, and this understanding is reciprocated; and it would not regard itself as out of communion with any members of the Free Church ecclesiastical families anywhere in the world. Full communion in all cases means mutual recognition of ministers and members and, in the case of Churches possessing the historic episcopate, the right of bishops of one Church to take part in the consecration of bishops in the other. Neither the Church of England nor the Methodist Church could contemplate breaking off at any point any of these relations of full communion that now exist.

The Methodist Stipulation

155 It will be recalled that when in 1953 the Methodist Conference indicated its readiness 'to proceed to a further stage in the promotion of intercommunion with the Church of England', it sought an assurance that 'the Methodist Church would be free to preserve the relations of intercommunion and fellowship with other non-episcopal Churches which it now enjoys'. A reply was given in 1955 in a statement prepared by Joint Committees of the Convocations of Canterbury and York and approved by both Convocations. The Committees agreed that the stipulation did 'not of itself raise an insuperable barrier to fruitful discussions with the Methodists'. They added, however, that 'the nature and extent of these "relations of intercommunion and fellowship" must be an important subject in any such discussions', and that, on the side of the Church of England, 'its own essential order and discipline would need to be safeguarded' (*Report*, pp. 7–8). It should be noted that the original context of the Methodist stipulation related to intercommunion, and also that the specific assurance sought in 1953 was not specifically given.

156 The Methodist Conference in 1955 accepted the reply as a basis for the Conversations which began in 1956. The present two-stage scheme for organic union emerged in the course of the Conversations. The original Methodist stipulation, strictly interpreted, relates to Stage One (full communion) for that was all that was envisaged in 1953. During Stage One, the stipulation will create no great difficulty. But it has become clear in the continuing debate that a much harder problem arises regarding the future of the 'relations of intercommunion and fellowship' now maintained by *both* Churches when Stage Two is reached.

157 The relations now maintained by the Church of England, as, for instance, with the Old Catholic Church, have been formally and officially negotiated and established. Those maintained by the Methodist Church have developed by custom in the course of time without specific formulation, and as a result are less precisely defined. It is desirable that their nature and extent should now be clarified, and we note that study of this matter was initiated by the 1967 Methodist Conference.

Stage Two

158 Many in both Churches, and especially members of the Methodist Church, are profoundly disturbed by the dissentient

judgement that the original Methodist stipulation 'has been met, and can be met, only for Stage One. When Stage Two is reached, Methodism will exist only as part of a new Church, and since this new Church can come into being only on the basis of the "strictest invariability" of episcopal ordination, it is very improbable that it will be in communion with non-episcopal Churches. Methodists will then no longer be in full communion with their reformed and evangelical brethren in the other Free Churches' (*Report*, p. 61).

159 The Church of England has not, so far, officially amplified or made more precise the tentative reply that helped to initiate the original discussions, though relevant comment may be expected from the Report of the Archbishops' Commission on Intercommunion and the debates which will follow its publication. The 1967 Methodist Conference received a Memorial asking for 'a further report at an early date showing in unambiguous terms the way in which the present full communion that exists between Methodism and other Churches outside the historic episcopate will be maintained in Stage Two of the Unity proposals'. The Conference replied: 'While this Conference cannot legislate for future Conferences, it reaffirms its conviction that no scheme of reunion should be considered which involves a severance of the Methodist Church from other Churches in this country or overseas with which it is already in full communion.'

A Developing Situation

160 It should be noted that, while Stage One has been described as the temporary acceptance of the existence of two *parallel* episcopal Churches, the mathematical phrase is not wholly accurate. There will in Stage One be two *convergent* Churches, growing together in mutual understanding through full communion and increasingly close co-operation and partnership. Stage Two will be negotiated out of this growing together. It would be presumptuous to assume that we can forecast in precise detail how the two Churches will then desire to become one.

161 Nor can we forecast with assurance the situation in which the final plans for entering Stage Two will be negotiated. We are living in a time of remarkable and rapid changes in relations between all Churches. All over the world there are church union schemes: some in the initial stages of preliminary discussion, some approaching the point of consummation, and some already carried through. Many of

them involve the participation of Anglicans and Methodists. A blue-print for Anglican–Methodist organic union drawn in 1968 would almost certainly need to be re-drawn long before Stage One had run its course.

New Roman Catholic Thinking about Intercommunion

162. A plan for union that erected barriers between those who have hitherto enjoyed the fellowship of full communion would give intolerable offence to the consciences of many Christians. A scheme that strengthened an existing barrier would be equally offensive. Apprehension of this second possibility underlies the anxieties of Anglicans who seek closer fellowship with the Church of Rome. It is noteworthy, however, that one result of the new Roman Catholic readiness to enter into ecumenical discussion has been a reappraisal of intercommunion. Commenting on the Decree on Ecumenism of the Second Vatican Council, section 15 of which favours Roman Catholic intercommunion with the Orthodox Churches as a means of expressing their present real, though incomplete, unity, and securing fuller unity for the future, the Roman Catholic Archbishop of Edessa has observed: 'As for the partial intercommunion that the Council has allowed between the two Churches, it certainly does not exclude dogmatic differences, but can contribute towards preparing the rapprochement.... In certain circumstances it answers the spiritual needs of some of the people who would otherwise be deprived of the fruits of the sacraments. On the other hand, it prepares the paths of unity by giving Catholics the opportunity to know and appreciate the Orthodox Church better. Intercommunion is undoubtedly the expression of unity of faith; but in the case of division, its continuance can prepare for reconciliation.'[1] This development in Roman Catholic thought must not be overlooked when gauging the effect of the present scheme on relations with the Roman Church.

All Existing Relations Must be Maintained Throughout

163 The main emphasis in debate has hitherto, understandably, been on the Methodist stipulation, but it should be noted that both Churches are rightly concerned to secure the maintenance of existing relations of fellowship and full communion. It should be recognized that the Churches with which relationships are at present maintained, whether by formalized agreement or by custom, will themselves

---

[1] *Eastern Churches Review*, Vol. 1, No. 1 (1966), p. 22.

properly be concerned with the decision that is ultimately made, and that account will need to be taken of their likely reactions. There are, moreover, many within the Church of England to whom any prospect of inter-celebration with Churches that do not possess the historic episcopate would present serious conscientious difficulties. The argument has centred on what may, or should, happen in Stage Two, but the significance of what happens in Stage One must not be overlooked. It is agreed that neither Church would be willing to enter on Stage One unless its existing relations with other Churches were maintained. This means that *both* our Churches, and those with which each is now in fellowship, will be accepting the fact that a Church possessing the historic episcopate and in full communion with the Church of England (Methodism in Stage One) will maintain a relationship of full communion with non-episcopal Churches.

164 Though any attempt to formulate now a detailed plan for organic union, including the details of intercommunion with other Churches, would be foolish, there is valuable guidance in the church union schemes in other parts of the world which include Anglicans and Methodists. Such schemes as that which resulted in the Church of South India, and those which are approaching fulfilment in Nigeria, Ghana, Ceylon, North India, and Pakistan, are based on proposals for organic union that are equivalent to our Stage Two. In every one of them known to us there is some such clause as that in the Plan of Church Union in North India and Pakistan: 'It is the intention of the Church of North India/Pakistan that full inter-communion and fellowship shall be maintained with each of the several Churches with which any of the uniting Churches was at the time of union in communion, and the fact that any of these does not follow the rule of episcopal ordination will not preclude the Church of North India/Pakistan from holding relations of communion and fellowship with it.'[1]

A Firm and Declared Intention

165 We are convinced that as our two Churches move forward into Stage One they should do so with the firm and declared intention that ways shall be found by which at Stage Two no relations at present maintained by either Church will be broken.

166 As things stand at present the requirement of the strictest in-variability of episcopal ordination, with its concomitant that the

[1] *The Plan of Church Union in North India and Pakistan*, p. 37, Fourth Revised Edition.

celebration of the Eucharist is confined to bishops and presbyters so ordained, cannot in a united Church be reconciled with a provision which allows the Holy Communion to be celebrated by visiting ministers who have not been episcopally ordained. This could cause an indefinite postponement of Stage Two. But since we believe it to be God's will that our Churches should unite, we must also believe that he will show us the right way through this difficulty. Progress towards unity among other Churches, and the changes of thought on the subject to which we have referred, justify our Churches in going forward without even a provisional solution to the problem before them. In Stage One they will remain autonomous, able freely to consider both by themselves and together the steps that will be needed in due course. As in mutual trust and common faith they pray and make their plans, we believe that the problem will be resolved.

8 Non-Participation in the Services of Reconciliation

The Standing of Non-participant Ministers in Their Own Churches

167 It seems more than likely that if the present scheme is accepted, a minority of Anglican and Methodist ministers will be unwilling, for conscientious reasons, to take part in the integration of ministries. This will mean that the relationship created by the Service will fall somewhat short of full communion in practice. However, respect for the conscience of the individual is of the essence of the scheme, and therefore this anomaly must be accepted without hesitation. No compensation could be adequate if a Church inhibited its own ministers from doing the work for which they were ordained, and it would be fallacious to think that every non-participant Anglican or Methodist minister could with a clear conscience transfer to another Church, or turn to secular work. No disabilities, therefore, will be imposed on these conscientious minorities, and their legal and ecclesiastical status will not be reduced by reason of their inability to accept this new departure in their Church's life. The Anglican clergyman's freehold, for instance, will not be affected, nor will the Methodist minister's right to appointment.

168 Those whose conscientious convictions are respected in this way may in turn be expected to honour the equally conscientious convictions of Anglicans and Methodists who believe the scheme to be right. A generous tolerance and trust will be maintained by all parties. Non-participant ministers will vary in their degree of willingness to practise such eucharistic fellowship with the other Church as is legally open to them, but this will not affect their standing as members of their own ministry, or the good will with which they are regarded. We are confident that they will in every case do all that their conscience allows to further the growth together of the two Churches during Stage One.

169 We urge that, if the scheme is accepted, the following steps should at once be taken:

(i) Both Churches should pledge themselves to seek adequate

spheres of service for all their non-participating ministers throughout Stage One.

(ii) Both Churches should make it clear that relations of fellowship which already exist between Methodist ministers and Anglican clergy (exchange of preachers, for instance) will not be affected adversely by non-participation in the integration of the ministries; and that where, for reasons of pastoral need, permission has already been given for ministers of either Church to conduct services in buildings belonging to the other, this will continue.

(iii) It should be accepted that the official lists of ministers published by, or for, the two Churches will not record whether or not individual ministers have taken part in the integration of the ministries. While those appointing clergy to parishes or stationing ministers in circuits will have to take account of each man's attitude to, and qualification for, the practice of eucharistic fellowship with the other Church, nothing must be done that would endanger the inward unity and fellowship of either ministry.

(iv) Both Churches should state that a non-participating minister who at a later stage wishes to receive the appropriate commissioning of the Services of Reconciliation may freely do so.

Lay Members who Dissent

170   In considering the position of non-participants the position of individual lay people is not less important than that of ordained ministers. There will be some who agree and some who do not agree with their present ministers; it is likely that some Anglican congregations and some Methodist societies will approach the practice of full communion with initial hesitation. This is one reason why the process of association at Stage One must not be hurried, and why all concerned should have time not only to consider the recommendations but to experience their outworking in the life of the Churches. Meanwhile, the conscientious scruples of all Anglicans and Methodists must in all cases be respected.

Clergy Withdrawing from Either Church at Stage One

171   It is our hope that no ministers will feel obliged to separate from their own Churches during Stage One. If, however, some should feel bound to withdraw, we are confident that each Church will, at the very least, make normal pension provision for them. Further help might be needed in particular cases to avoid hardship to a man's

dependants, and this should not be grudged. We urge that the pension authorities of the two Churches should at an early stage consider the means by which this might be achieved. The same principles should apply to any who feel conscientiously bound to resign from the ministry when Stage Two is inaugurated.

General

172 This chapter has been written in an attempt to state the principles which we consider should guide both Churches in their attempt to work out how the majority and the dissentients can be fair to each other. We would repeat, with emphasis, that the fullest generosity in respecting each other's consciences, and the greatest good will in accepting anomalies of practice, are at this point vital. In the processes involved in the healing of our divisions we must seek under the guidance of the Holy Spirit to do what is right, not only for our Churches as a whole but also for those who, for conscience' sake, are caught up in positions of particular difficulty. The inner unity of our present Churches and their ministries is ours to hold in trust for the united Church that is to come, and no pains can be too great for us to take in order to preserve this unity intact.

9 Growing Together in Stage One

Introduction: Some Apprehensions

173 The united Church at Stage Two will be, quite clearly, neither exactly the Church of England as it now is, nor exactly the Methodist Church as it now is—still less what either might become in continued isolation. The two Churches will have been fused into a community in which the heritage of each will be integrated with that of the other, to make possible a new manifestation of the life of God's people. In Stage One the two Churches will be growing together in preparation for receiving this divine gift.

174 As they enter Stage One, many of their members will be brought into closer contact than ever before with customs, traditions, and ways of thought and worship which are unfamiliar to them. This prospect, quite naturally, is causing some apprehension, and the fear that when Methodists and Anglicans come really near together, they will find differences between the Churches which will make them regret the step towards unity which they have taken. Others, again, in both Churches are prevented from giving full assent to the proposals for union, not by theological reasons, but by dislike of what they believe to happen in the other Church.

175 Some Methodists, for instance, are wary of having close links with an established Church. They speak of it as 'tied up with the State'. Others object to what they call the 'set forms' and 'constant repetitions' of the Anglican liturgy; others have formed the impression that the clergyman has too much power, and say things like 'the parson rules the roost, and the layman does not get a look-in'. Some members of the Church of England, on the other hand, are doubtful of the itinerant system of the Methodist ministry which seems to rob a congregation of its pastor much too frequently, and sometimes for apparently arbitrary reasons; others dislike what they call the 'free and easy atmosphere' of Methodist worship, and the extemporary prayers which seem to characterize it and to be excessively long; others are fearful of the 'undue centralization' of which they have heard rumours.

Some Assurances

176   The relations of the Church of England, and the future united Church, with the State are of very great importance, and are discussed at length in Chapter 15. It may suffice to say here that Methodist fears of 'State control' are unfounded, and that the Church of England is considering once again its relationship with the State, including those aspects of it which Methodists find unacceptable. In the other matters mentioned above the differences between the two Churches are much less than once they were, and in every case the Churches are steadily becoming more like each other. For instance, in the matter of worship, Methodist Churches use ordered liturgies far more than they did, while services in the Church of England display a much greater variety.

177   The witness of each Church in matters of social and personal ethics has in the past been mostly concerned with different issues and contained different emphases. But here also a natural process of assimilation is going on, and the officers of the Church of England's Board of Social Responsibility and the Methodist Church's Department of Christian Citizenship are already working out a common programme. In fact, in all matters which affect the Churches' witness to society, the custom is well established by which the committees of both Churches, at national, regional, and local level, invite observers to each other's discussions.

178   Matters relating to Baptism and Confirmation (or Reception into Full Membership) occupy Chapter 11. Differences in marriage discipline are fully discussed in Chapter 12. Certain matters of practice relating to Holy Communion, and therefore touching the very centre of the Churches' life, are dealt with in the remainder of this chapter.

Lay Celebration (or Administration)

179   A verbal problem faces us at the outset: the word 'administration', as used in relation to Holy Communion, has one meaning for a Methodist and another for an Anglican. 'Administration' in Methodist usage is equivalent to the Anglican 'celebration'. To avoid this confusion we shall use these words in the Anglican way. Though this involves frequent translation of official Methodist terminology, it is, in our judgement, essential in order to keep clear the distinction between 'lay administration' and 'lay celebration'. If this distinction is recognized, the apparent wide divergence between Anglican and

Methodist practice is seen to be considerably narrowed. Lay persons in the Church of England may be authorized to assist the celebrant in the distribution of the elements to the people, and lay administration in this sense is increasing. This is wholly congruous with the Methodist practice whereby lay people occasionally distribute the elements.

180 In Anglican usage the celebrant, or president, at the Lord's Table is always a bishop or priest. In Methodist usage the celebrant is normally an ordained minister, but exceptions to the clearly stated general rule[1] may be approved where it can be shown that a congregation would otherwise be deprived of reasonably regular and frequent celebrations. Each such 'dispensation' is for a named individual and for a specified circuit, and lasts at a maximum for three years only, after which it may be renewed. It is granted only with the express approval of all the courts of the Church: Circuit Quarterly Meeting, District Synod, and Conference. Dispensations are given to some deaconesses who exercise a pastoral ministry and have the care of souls. Annual dispensations are given to most probationer ministers. Very few applications, other than for probationer ministers or deaconesses, are made or approved.[2]

181 From the beginning of Stage One it should be recognized as a principle that thereafter the celebration of the Holy Communion is to be confined to bishops and presbyters (*Report*, pp. 48 and 55), but it must be recognized also that the special conditions which have been held to justify lay celebration in the Methodist Church may not immediately disappear everywhere. This will involve a limitation on the extent of intercommunion between the two Churches and should therefore be brought to an end as soon as possible.

182 We recommend therefore that, after entry on Stage One, no dispensation for a circuit should be granted to any person (including a probationer minister or deaconess) who does not already hold one for that circuit. The dispensations for those already authorized should be carefully reviewed at the statutory intervals in the light of local conditions then prevailing. We realize that this will cause considerable temporary difficulty for some circuits. We are confident never-

[1] 'The general usage of the three uniting Churches whereby the Sacrament of the Lord's Supper is administered by Ministers shall continue to be observed' (*CPD*, p. 4).

[2] There are 11,500 Methodist preaching places. At July 1966, twenty-eight laymen, including six retired lay pastors, held dispensations. Of 235 Wesley Deaconesses in active work, thirty-six held dispensations.

theless that, as our two Churches grow together, sacramental needs will be amply met by their common presbyteral ministry, and that the conditions which have made dispensations necessary will soon be removed.

The Reverent Disposal of Consecrated Elements

183   After considering this question in considerable detail we have come to the firm conclusion that it is not possible for us to specify a uniform method for disposing of unconsumed consecrated elements at the close of services of Holy Communion in the Methodist Church. We understand that in the draft proposals for the new Methodist Book of Offices it is likely that there will be a rubric in the Holy Communion service to the effect that 'the bread and wine remaining after the service shall be disposed of with reverence, as determined by the Minister in consultation with the Poor Stewards'.[1] We believe that such a rubric will be welcomed by members of the Methodist Church, and by those members of the Church of England who have expressed a proper concern that the elements should not be carelessly or irreverently handled. The proposed Methodist rubric will give the minister the responsibility of ensuring this.

184   The question of the disposal of the elements also arises for discussion in the Church of England, because of the widespread adoption of the westward position of the celebrant. We commend the procedure laid down in the Book of Worship of the Church of South India[2] to the careful consideration of both Churches, and point out that those who favour such a procedure as this do not thereby imply a particular theological interpretation of the sacramental presence of Christ.

The Use of Fermented Wine

185   This is a particularly difficult matter, for the considered judgements of the two Churches, as expressed in Canon Law and Methodist Standing Orders, are diametrically opposed. It is also an immediate matter, for the question of the nature of the wine to be used is

[1] The 'Poor Stewards' in Methodism are the stewards of 'the fund for the poor', a collection for whom is regularly taken at Holy Communion. They are also responsible for seeing that the Table is duly prepared for the service.

[2] *After the benediction the ministers go out, carrying with them the Bible, the gifts of the people, and the vessels used for the Communion. Any bread or wine set apart in the service which remains over is carried out to the vestry, and there is reverently consumed* (The Book of Common Worship, p. 20).

raised by the Services of Reconciliation themselves, of which Holy Communion is an integral part.

186 The Anglican Canon insists that the wine must be 'a pure fermented juice of the grape'. The central argument is that the wine used by our Lord at the Last Supper was of this nature.

187 All denominations which came together to form the Methodist Church had been deeply involved since the middle of the nineteenth century in the total abstinence movement. It was held that in the struggle against what many felt to be the most urgent social problem of the day the Church should have no complicity with the drink trade, and, as a logical extension of this view, that a source of so much contemporary misery should not be honoured by use on the Lord's Table. The fundamental reason for the Methodist Standing Order, therefore, was, and remains, a social one.

188 The underlying argument has never been carried to its logical extreme. On the contrary, the Conference Declaration on Total Abstinence plainly states that 'the Conference has not at any time imposed total abstinence from the use of intoxicating liquors as a condition of membership of the Methodist Church'. It should be added that many Methodists who are convinced total abstainers do not hold that they would deny their convictions if the wine they received at Holy Communion were fermented.

189 From Methodist Union until 1966 the relevant Standing Order ruled that 'the wine used shall be unfermented'. In conformity with the pre-1966 Standing Order the 'wines' normally used in Methodism were:

(a) A non-alcoholic product, commercially produced, made from sugar, water, and fruit essence.
(b) A diluted fruit syrup.
(c) A pure grape juice.

The Conference of 1966 substituted 'non-alcoholic' for 'unfermented'—a slight but significant change which permits the use of a comparatively new product, a true wine (fermented grape juice) from which alcohol has been removed.

190 We suggest that by emendation of the relevant Standing Order 305 (1) the Methodist Church should agree that the juice of the grape shall be used. We understand that a rubric to this effect is likely to appear in the draft proposals for the Service of Holy Communion in

the new Methodist Book of Offices. In support of our recommendation we draw attention to the importance of the imagery of the vine in both the Old and New Testaments.

191 Methodists do not insist that Anglicans must use unfermented wine in the Eucharist, and it would be wrong for Anglicans to insist that from the outset of Stage One Methodists must use fermented alcoholic wine. It would be a tragedy if this issue prevented or marred our coming together. Each Church must be willing, for the sake of the greater good, to begin Stage One by respecting the usages of the other; thus leaving the way open for the continuing amicable debate that is necessary before Stage Two.

192 The Services of Reconciliation should reflect the greatest possible measure of agreement and mutual understanding. We recommend that the wine used at these Services should be the pure juice of the grape.

Open Communion

193 The Order of Service for Holy Communion in the Methodist Book of Offices is derived from, and is substantially similar to, the Order in the Book of Common Prayer. In both Churches the invitation to participate is addressed to those who 'truly and earnestly repent of their sins, and are in love and charity with their neighbours, and intend to lead a new life, following the commandments of God, and walking from henceforth in his holy ways'.

194 The rubric at the end of the Order of Confirmation in the Book of Common Prayer states: 'And there shall none be admitted to the holy Communion, until such time as he be confirmed, or be ready and desirous to be confirmed.' There is diversity of interpretation of this rubric within the Church of England. In some parishes it is held not to exclude a general invitation to communicant members of other Churches to receive Communion in the Church of England. The Resolutions of the Upper Houses of the Convocations in 1933 appear to have regarded the rubric as exclusive. These Resolutions provided for exceptions to the rule in the case of colleges and schools, gatherings designed to promote Christian unity, and members of other Churches cut off for a period from the ministrations of their own Church. They are generally taken as the standard of practice. (They have recently been re-examined by the Archbishops' Commission on Intercommunion, whose Report is awaited as we write.) No one who presents himself is likely to be repelled from the Table, but if some-

one who is not confirmed wishes to present himself regularly, though he is not prevented by distance from communicating in a Church of his own communion, he will be encouraged to seek confirmation.

195 In Methodism it was for a long time the established custom to admit to Holy Communion only those who showed class tickets, or notes of admission from the minister, which were granted to members of other communions. This procedure was gradually relaxed, and it is now a widespread practice to invite to Holy Communion not only members of the Methodist Church and members of other Churches, but 'all those who love the Lord Jesus Christ'. The invitation to participate is construed in terms of the call to all those who truly and earnestly repent of their sins, in the order of service itself. The practice of issuing this invitation is highly valued by many Methodists, as a witness to the universality of the gospel and the readiness of the Lord Jesus Christ to receive repentant sinners.

196 These divergent practices can be reconciled when the two Churches are in communion with each other, if (a) Methodist ministers invite to Holy Communion those who are members of the Methodist Church or of any Church with which the Methodist Church is in communion, and those who love the Lord Jesus Christ and who, having been baptized, wish to show by coming to the Lord's Table their repentance and their desire to be prepared for reception into full membership of the Church, or confirmation; and (b) the Church of England recognizes this practice as legitimate. In this way the dual concern for the Sacrament as a sign both of incorporation into the Body of Christ, and of God's universal love for sinners, will be recognized and expressed.

APPENDIX:
THE DIACONATE

197 The third order of the historic threefold ministry is that of deacon. In the West it became in course of time a probationary order leading to the priesthood. It still performs this function, but of late the Church of Rome, in common with some provinces of the Anglican Communion, has ordained deacons who are not expected to proceed to the priesthood. Their ministry is primarily pastoral and evangelistic rather than sacramental, though it includes the liturgical functions proper to a deacon of reading Scripture in the church and assisting in the distribution of the consecrated elements at Holy Communion.

It is too early to judge whether this revival of a permanent diaconate will prove to be a fruitful development in ministry for the Church's work today, but the Commission draws attention to the fact that several of the lay orders which have arisen in the life of our two Churches appear to be fulfilling many of the historic functions of the deacon. It was for this reason that we made our second recommendation in paragraphs 201-2 below.

Reprinted from Chapter 5 of *Towards Reconciliation*

The Present

198 It appears that the Methodist probationer minister is very nearly the exact equivalent of the Anglican deacon. We think it desirable that, as our two ministries are to be assimilated to one another in the episcopate and the presbyterate, this assimilation should be carried to its logical conclusion in the diaconate also.

199 This would have the advantage of removing a possible source of friction and debate: the probationary ministries in the two Churches would be for all practical purposes identical in status, duties, and functions.

200 We therefore suggest that the Methodist Church should consider whether, from the beginning of Stage One, Methodist candidates for the presbyterate should, upon leaving college, be made deacons according to the form provided in the new Ordinal which both Churches will use.

The Future

201 Further, we recommend that the two Churches, preferably in consultation with theologians of other Christian bodies, should initiate a thorough study and assessment of the present lay orders of ministry in relation to the historic order of deacon.

202 This, we believe, ought to involve:

(a) A study of the history of the order of deacon.

(b) Consideration of the present use of that order.

(c) Consideration of whether there is, or is not, a need for a full-time and permanent order of liturgical and pastoral ministry supplementary to that of the presbyterate, such as exists, for instance, in the Church of England in the Church Army captain.

(d) Consideration of whether a lay ministry which regularly conducts public worship and preaches (for example, Lay Readers in the Church of England, and Local Preachers in the Methodist Church) ought not to be recognized as being in that degree a 'holy' order, and be ordained to it.

(e) Consideration of the place of the order of deaconess in both Churches. For example, is the order necessarily to be regarded as *sui generis*, as it is at present? Or would it be right to envisage the establishment of an order of deacon which should be open to both men and women?

10 Lay Ministries

Introduction

203 In comments upon the 1963 Report the question of lay ministries was several times raised in one form or another. Some aspects of this, lay celebration of Holy Communion, for example, and the relationship of ministerial priesthood to the priesthood of the whole Church, are dealt with elsewhere: here we are concerned with lay ministries in general, and with the particular lay ministries to be found in our two Churches.

204 The whole concept of ministry is today under continuous discussion and debate, and this will certainly go on. This chapter examines the present practice of our two Churches, and makes suggestions as to how the work which we are at present doing in separation may come to be done together. In fellowship with one another we shall see more clearly what new patterns of ministry God is showing to his Church in the present age.

205 It should be said at the outset that, although the particular points raised in comment on the 1963 Report were chiefly concerned with specific lay ministries, our two Churches must, in our judgement, be at least equally concerned with that call to ministry which rests upon the whole people of God. Otherwise there is serious danger of clericalizing the ministry of lay people, so that it is thought of primarily as an adjunct to the ordained ministry, instead of in terms of its more proper role in the world outside the Christian community, the world where the Church is called to serve all men for Christ's sake. On this see paragraphs 226–7 below.

The Background

206 The tradition of the Church of England and of the Methodist Church is that an ordained ministry of word and sacrament which also possesses pastoral commission and authority in the Church is in accordance with the mind of Christ and with the continuous history and practice of the Church. That is to say, the whole *laos*, or people of God, can be subdivided into the clergy and the laity. Our present ministerial organization is based upon this distinction, and it is from this basis that we must begin.

207   However, in spite of the long-established distinction between the clergy and the laity, other recognized forms of 'orders' or ministry, in addition to the 'holy' orders, have existed in the Church from earliest times. An example is to be found in the traditional 'minor' orders of subdeacon, reader, exorcist, acolyte, etc. The monastic orders, too, which are not confined to priests, but also include lay-brothers and sisters, provide another instance of recognized lay ministries.

THE CHURCH OF ENGLAND

Religious Communities

208   In the Church of England, however, the minor orders and the monastic orders disappeared at the Reformation, and recognized lay ministries (with the exception of lay members of choral foundations, parish clerks, etc.) did not emerge again until the middle of the nineteenth century, when religious orders for both men and women began to reappear. There are in the Church of England today nine such orders for men, mainly consisting of priests but usually including lay-brothers as well,[1] and over forty for women.

Readers

209   In 1866 a lay order of 'reader' was revived, and has since become an accepted and widely used ministry, part-time and unpaid, and generally comparable to that of the local preacher in Methodism. A reader may read Morning and Evening Prayer (except for the absolution and the blessing, which are reserved to the priest), preach sermons, and by specific authority from the bishop assist in the distribution of the consecrated elements at Holy Communion in a particular parish. He cannot, however, officiate without licence from the bishop in whose diocese he is serving, whether his ministry is limited to a specific parish (in which case he is called a 'parochial reader'), or extends to the whole diocese (in which case he is called a 'diocesan reader').

210   Though the Church of England does not depend upon its readers to so great a degree as Methodism depends upon its local preachers, it would be impossible to maintain the regular Sunday worship of the Church of England in many places, particularly in

---

[1] For example, according to recently published figures, the Society of the Sacred Mission (Kelham) consists of forty-nine priests and twenty-six lay-brothers.

country districts, without the help of these lay ministers. The Convocations have recently authorized the opening of this ministry to women.

The Church Army

211 In 1882 the Reverend Wilson Carlile founded the Church Army on the model of the Salvation Army. The captains and sisters of the Church Army hold the office of 'lay evangelist'. Their work is full-time and paid, and covers a wide variety of service in parochial work, social work, etc. With the licence of the bishop, they may conduct public worship in the same way as a licensed reader.

The Order of Deaconesses

212 In 1861 the Bishop of London revived the Order of Deaconesses. This order has continued in the Church of England during the past century. It is the one order of ordained ministry for women in the Church of England. A deaconess may, with the bishop's licence, conduct Morning and Evening Prayer (except those parts reserved to the priest) and preach the sermon. Although the order is entered by ordination, it ranks as a lay, rather than a clerical, ministry, in that its members are eligible for election to the House of Laity in the Church Assembly, but not to the House of Clergy. Nevertheless, ordination to it is held to be for life. (It is interesting to note that the Wesley Deaconess Order shares with it this ambivalent nature.) It is a full-time, paid ministry.

213 There is in the Church of England one community of professed religious sisters living under rule, all of whom are also ordained deaconesses, namely the Deaconess Community of St Andrew.

Women Workers

214 Another recognized ministry for women in the Church of England is that of licensed woman worker. Such women have to take an authorized course of training, usually residential, leading to the award of a recognized qualification, the 'Inter-Diocesan Certificate'. They serve in various capacities, but the majority are on the staff of a parish, under licence from the bishop. The work is full-time and paid, but there is no necessary intention of lifelong commitment to this ministry. It is this fact which chiefly distinguishes it from the Deaconess Order.

215 These recognized lay ministries in the Church of England have arisen pragmatically, rather than as the result of a centrally considered policy.

THE METHODIST CHURCH

Local Preachers

216 Early Methodism owed much to the band of preachers who shared in John Wesley's work. Some of these who were able to serve full-time and who, like Wesley himself, were continually travelling, were called 'itinerant preachers'. Others, bound by ties of work and family to one locality, became 'local preachers'. From the former group comes the present ordained ministry of Methodism; from the latter, the order of local preachers.

217 Throughout the nineteenth century the number of local preachers steadily grew. They became a distinctive feature of Methodism, which could not have survived without them. Today, three out of four Methodist services are conducted by local preachers, a number of whom are women. A fully accredited local preacher, approved after examination and testing as a 'preacher on trial' by the circuit in which he resides, is accepted as a local preacher throughout the Methodist Church, and is not required to seek fresh authority to preach when moving to a new circuit or District.

The Wesley Deaconess Order

218 The only full-time accredited order of ministry for women in the Methodist Church is that of the Wesley Deaconess Order, founded in 1890. During this century it has increasingly become the practice to admit women as local preachers, and since the last war nearly all candidates for the Wesley Deaconess Order have been, or have become, local preachers.

219 Not infrequently they have oversight of local Methodist congregations. Though ordained to the Order, they rank among the laity in the Methodist Conference.

Class Leaders

220 Class leaders form a lay ministry which shares with the ordained minister the pastoral care of church members. This system was developed by John Wesley to maintain pastoral care of the scattered

groups converted under his preaching. It has proved of great and lasting value by providing that every church member can look for guidance and help not only to his minister, but also to a fellow-member of wisdom and experience who is charged with a measure of spiritual responsibility for him.

221 Traditionally, each class leader meets his members (not more than twelve in number) at a weekly meeting in which they share their Christian experience. Today, in fact, many leaders do not meet their classes, but keep in touch with their members by visiting them at least once a quarter, or by meeting them at church. The class leaders form the nucleus of the local pastoral committee or 'smaller Leaders' Meeting', which deals with discipline and annually reviews the names on the membership roll. Though there is nothing precisely corresponding to class leaders in the Church of England, they have some similarity to street wardens or leaders of house groups in some Anglican parishes.

Points of Similarity

222 The two points at which the Church of England and the Methodist Church most nearly correspond to one another in lay ministry are the orders of reader and of local preacher, and the two orders of deaconess—with which should be conjoined that of licensed woman worker in the Church of England.

223 The present life and work of our two Churches are heavily dependent upon these ministries, and are not likely to be less so in the foreseeable future. We confidently expect that there will be increasing co-operation and a considerable degree of interchange between our two Churches as far as these ministries are concerned. This will provide a fruitful area for our growing together in Stage One, and we ask the authorities of our two Churches to take formal steps to make it possible, and to encourage it.

Training

224 With the exception of Methodist class leaders, it is required of the lay orders which we have enumerated that its members undergo some specific training and satisfy competent authorities of their intellectual and practical proficiency. Methods and standards of training are somewhat similar in the two Churches, and we note with satisfaction that the departments of our two Churches which

are concerned with these ministries are already in close touch with one another.[1] We hope that this will continue, and develop further.

Women in Holy Orders

225 A joint committee, appointed by the Archbishops of Canterbury and York and the President of the Methodist Conference, is at present examining the question whether women, who at present can exercise only lay ministries, should be admitted to the ordained ministry of the word and sacrament.

Ministry and the People of God

226 Our immediate concern has been with those more formal orders of ministry which have arisen to supplement the ordained ministry of the clergy in the conducting of public worship and in pastoral duty. This does not mean that we have not been conscious and appreciative of the work and the value of many other forms of lay ministry in both Churches: churchwardens, parochial church councillors, sidesmen, servers, members of choirs, stewards, teachers of children, leaders of youth groups, and others. Without this voluntary service in the parishes and circuits the pattern of our church life, pastoral and administrative, could not continue.

227 It must be repeated, however, that such service, and the more systematized orders of lay ministry which we have considered, are not the only, or the most necessary, forms in which lay members of the Church exercise a ministry. The primary ministry of lay people is to society at large. Secular occupations are Christian service, and need to be carried out as seriously and responsibly as any other religious duties. Christian thinking, Christian responsibility, and Christian action are concerned with the political, social, and economic structures of human society. On these things men's response, or lack of response, to the gospel often depends. Here lies the main sphere of Christian lay activity. As our two Churches come to live, to think, and to worship together, we shall gain a new understanding of lay mission and lay discipline. Then the people of God will be equipped to serve the world which Christ redeemed not only with more devotion, but also with more understanding and effectiveness.

[1] A useful booklet, *Local Preachers and Readers*, has been produced jointly by the Local Preachers' Department of the Methodist Church, 1 Central Buildings, S.W. 1, and by the Central Readers' Board of the Church of England, 45 Great Peter Street, S.W. 1, price 3*d*., plus postage.

228 NOTE. One of the subjects referred to us by the Methodist Conference was 'the participation of the laity in the Councils of the Church'. In view of the publication of the Church of England Report on Synodical Government and the considerable changes now under discussion in the Church of England, we do not think it desirable to make separate recommendations of our own under this head.

11 Baptism and Confirmation

A. THE PROBLEM OF
BAPTISMAL REGENERATION

Introduction

229 The signatories of 'A Dissentient View' anticipated that the statements of the 1963 Report on baptismal regeneration might cause 'some disquiet' through lack of precise definition (p. 61). 'The theological implications of infant baptism, including baptismal regeneration' was among the topics remitted to the Commission by the Methodist Conference. We believe that the various views about infant baptism which are current in both our Churches fall within the formularies of both. The following paragraphs, however, working afresh over the ground covered in the 1963 Report, will show that there is enough common thinking in both our Churches to secure from the outset of Stage One a harmony of pastoral and evangelistic practice in relation to infant baptism, and the subsequent reception of the baptized into full membership.

The Gospel

230 The gospel is the good news of God's saving action towards men. It 'proclaims the redemption, reconciliation, and re-creation wrought by God in Christ' (*Report*, p. 20). Hereby it exposes the state of man without Christ as being one of bondage to sin and estrangement from God, a state which the Bible calls death.

231 'From the standpoint of the individual it [the gospel] turns on justification by the free grace of Christ, received by faith' (loc. cit.). The gospel calls for personal trust in, and commitment to, the crucified and risen Jesus as Saviour and Lord, and offers salvation to those who believe in him. So the gospel is addressed to every individual person; it distinguishes each man from the mass, demanding that he respond to Christ for himself. But God's call through the gospel also unites, for the grace that justifies, reconciles, and re-creates, at the same time incorporates into the body of Christ, which is the covenant people of God and the community that partakes of the Holy Spirit. In this sense, as the Report says, 'throughout the New Testament,

justification by faith has corporate no less than individual reference' (loc. cit.). To be in Christ is to be in his Church. Insistence on individual conversion, and recognition that the Christian life is essentially corporate, so far from being opposed, are complementary and correlative; for only those who have found true individuality and freedom through faith-union with Jesus Christ are qualified to share the life of tireless service and outreach to which the Church is called. 'Therefore, in any account of the Church, grace, faith, conversion, freedom, will have their full place' (loc. cit.).

Regeneration and Baptism

232   The New Testament uses the images of 'rebirth', being 'born again', 'brought to birth', 're-begotten', 'begotten of God' (see Titus 3. 5; John 3. 3-8; Jas. 1. 18; 1 Pet. 1. 3, 23; 1 John 2. 29; 3. 9; 5. 1, 4) to indicate that the event of conversion, which includes illumination, repentance towards God, and faith 'into' Jesus Christ, involves a divine work of inward renewal. St Paul calls it our quickening, our co-resurrection with Christ, and our new creation in him (Eph. 2. 1-10; 2 Cor. 5. 17), and links it explicitly with baptism in Rom. 6. 1-11 and Col. 2. 10-12.

233   Christian theologians have not been unanimous in their definitions of regeneration, nor in their judgements as to how far the word may be used as a technical term, and different views on these points are found in both our Churches.

234   All would agree, however, that regeneration is connected with personal newness of life, that this is necessary for salvation, and that there is no warrant for describing as regenerate those adults who show no sign of repentance or faith.

235   The 'fairly representative' Methodist statement on the sacraments, printed in the Report as evidence of closeness of thinking in this field in both Churches, describes baptism as a dominical sacrament conveying the gospel, and requiring to be received 'by faith which is a response to the gospel that is proclaimed and involves a confession of Christ as Saviour and Lord' (*Report*, p. 30). Baptism is a sign of regeneration through union with Christ, and also of cleansing and repentance, through the work of the Holy Spirit. As such, baptism admits to the fellowship of the Church, which is Christ's body and flock.

236   From this it follows that, while the potency of baptism as a means of grace rests upon the reality of the redemption wrought by

Christ and the promised operation of God's free Spirit, baptism must be appropriated by its recipients and issue in personal newness of life if it is finally to benefit them. Baptism requires conversion, for the baptismal life is a life of sustained repentance and faith, whereby regeneration is manifest. These positions are common ground to all in both our Churches.

Infant Baptism

237 'Both our Churches regard the baptism of infants as a legitimate development of the teaching of the New Testament' (Report, p. 30). The infants in view are those whose parents or sponsors have themselves been baptized and undertake to give the children a Christian upbringing. Of each such infant when baptized, the 1662 office of Publick Baptism declares: 'Seeing now...that this Child is regenerate.' This phrase, which is not found either in the present Methodist Service of Holy Baptism, or in the Service authorized by the Methodist Conference in 1967 for experimental use, is not understood by all Anglicans in the same way. Some would expound this 'baptismal regeneration' in terms of God's gracious conveyance, by sign and seal, of a promise of new life, on which the faith of the parents, the Church, and, in due course, the child must lay hold; other Anglicans would expound it in terms of an 'operation of grace in unconscious processes which may find their fruition in faith and love' (Report, p. 31). Neither of these views implies that the child has by baptism already been finally assured of eternal life. The two views are not in any case mutually exclusive. Both are held in the Methodist Church, although the term regeneration is not often used in this connection.

238 The Commission believes that all Anglicans would accept John Wesley's insistence that unconverted adults baptized in infancy must be summoned to personal repentance and faith, and warned that without these baptism will not save them. Anglicans generally would also concur with the following paragraph in the Statement of the Methodist Conference on Holy Baptism (1952):

> Though the child baptized in infancy is an heir to the promises of God, he does not always or inevitably claim his inheritance.... He must see his sin and his need. He must put all his trust and confidence in Christ, both for his life here and for his hope of life everlasting. This full response, this saving faith, he cannot produce in his own unaided strength. It is the work of God, the Holy Spirit, and is essential to life in Christ. Whether this work is called 'Conversion', or 'the New Birth', whether it is regarded as sudden or gradual, or as both process and crisis, it is true that without the gift of saving

faith those baptized in infancy can never attain to their privileged life as sons of God. While Methodists recognize that Christ is the true Minister in Baptism and that therein Christ sets the child in the company of His people, they also declare that the personal appropriation of the promises of Christ by the child should be prayed for and expected.[1]

239 Equally the Commission believes that all in both Churches recognize the claim of baptized children upon the love and prayers of the congregation, and the need for them to be instructed in the gospel and to be led to the point of personal faith in Jesus Christ.

240 The Commission judges that, whatever detailed differences of view may remain, there is here sufficient basis as our two Churches grow together for a full integration of pastoral and theological practice in relation to baptism, and for the common exploration of the problems of pastoral care.

B. THE PRACTICE OF CHRISTIAN INITIATION

The Administration of Baptism

241 The official practice of both Churches concerning baptism, confirmation, reception into full membership, and first communion has been carefully reviewed by the Commission.

242 Both Churches are agreed that the sacrament of baptism is the foundation of Church membership. Article XXV of the Church of England states that Holy Baptism was ordained by Christ, and that it is an 'effectual sign of grace'. The Catechism states that the sacrament is 'generally necessary to salvation'. Parents are to bring their children to baptism as soon as possible after birth. Great care is taken that no one shall be presented for confirmation or receive Communion or Holy Orders unless he has previously been baptized. The invitation to Holy Communion of those from other Churches is confined to baptized communicants in good standing.

243 In the Methodist Church, the *Deed of Union* declares that 'the Methodist Church recognizes...baptism...as of divine appointment and of perpetual obligation, of which it is the privilege and duty of members to avail themselves'. The official *Statement on Holy*

[1] *MBM*, p. 24.

Baptism received by the Conference of 1952 states that 'a solemn obligation rests upon parents to present their children to Christ in Baptism...whereby they are joined to the visible community of God's people'.[1] The words quoted first appeared in the Statement on Infant Baptism of the Conference of 1936. No one can be received into full membership in the Methodist Church (let alone ordained) unless he has been previously baptized. We find, therefore, that there is substantial agreement as to the necessity of Holy Baptism in both Churches.

244 The normal minister of baptism in both our Churches is an ordained minister, and the normal service used is that provided in the Prayer Book and in the Methodist Book of Offices. A new Service was authorized for experimental use by the Methodist Conference in 1967, and the Anglican experimental service has been authorized also. Both Churches provide that baptism shall normally be administered during a service of public worship, in the presence of the congregation; though this provision is at present more frequently observed in the Methodist Church than in the Church of England. In cases of emergency, both Churches allow a lay person to administer the sacrament, using water and the name of the Trinity in the prescribed way.

Confirmation and Reception into Full Membership

245 There is common agreement that the baptism of infants, as practised by our two Churches, does not by itself fully represent the pattern of Christian initiation in the New Testament, where public profession of repentance and faith on the part of the candidates is also required. This is provided in the Church of England by confirmation, and in the Methodist Church by the service entitled 'Public Reception into Full Membership, or Confirmation'. In both Churches a period of intensive instruction and preparation is undertaken before candidates are presented. In both Churches a Catechism is available for this purpose, and the course normally includes instruction on the Creed and the duties and privileges of church membership. Further, in both Churches confirmation or reception into full membership is normally followed by first communion.

246 In addition to these public signs of conscious response there is a further element in the total act of initiation, as it has come down to us from the undivided Church: namely, invocation of the Spirit of God. This is represented in the Eastern Church by the anointing of

[1] *MBM*, p. 20.

the candidates by the priest with oil, accompanied by prayer for the Holy Spirit; and this anointing is administered to infants as part of the baptismal act. In the West confirmation became separated from the baptism of infants, and is administered later. In the Church of England it takes the form of the laying on of hands by the bishop with prayer that the gifts and graces already given in baptism may be confirmed and increased by the Holy Spirit. In the official *Report on Church Membership* adopted by the Methodist Conference in 1961, it is stated that 'this element is not brought into sufficient prominence by the present service for the Reception into Full Membership', and the desire is expressed that 'any revision of the Book of Offices should pay careful attention to this point, in the light of Methodist experience of inward religion, of personal awareness of Christ, and of the work of the Holy Spirit in the believer'.[1] In accordance with this the Service of Reception into Full Membership or Confirmation (authorized for experimental use by the Conference of 1967) gives much greater emphasis to the objective side of the rite.

247   These two consequential acts—the individual conscious response in faith to Christ's saving work, and the laying on of hands with prayer, for the fullness of the Holy Spirit, are not to be regarded as separate from the baptismal act, but as integral to it.

The Suggested Joint Service of Confirmation

248   The hope was expressed in the Convocation Report of 1965 that our Commission 'would consider the possibility of producing a common form of service for use in both Churches during Stage One, in which would be combined the Anglican tradition of episcopal laying on of hands, together with the strong elements of committal to personal discipleship to be found in the Methodist Order of Service for the Public Reception of New Members' (R, p. 13). The Commission gave careful and sympathetic consideration to this proposal. It found, however, that, as has been stated, the Church of England Liturgical Commission and the Methodist Faith and Order Committee had both recently produced new services of baptism and confirmation, and had consulted each other while doing so. The new Methodist services and the Anglican baptism and confirmation services have been authorized for experimental use. In the light of this, we were advised that it would be better that these new services, which have much in common, should be submitted to the Churches rather than that a third new joint service should be issued at this point.

[1] *MBM*, p. 34, n. 1.

We believe that the use of these new services will of itself draw our Churches closer together, and pave the way for the eventual production of a common service acceptable to us all.

Common Problems and Concerns

249 Both Churches are facing grave difficulties in the shepherding and after-care of baptized infants and confirmed young people, and both are experiencing a grievous falling away of baptized members. Greater effort is needed not only to integrate the candidates into the worshipping fellowship of the Church, but also to make them realize their full responsibility as Christians in the world. Critical examination of the theology and practice of Christian initiation is proceeding in both Churches as part of a wider ecumenical inquiry. New patterns of thought and practice are emerging. But neither Church is likely to find a satisfactory solution to its difficulties in isolation. We are confident that the shared experience of our two Churches during Stage One will strengthen both, in this field as elsewhere.

Remaining Differences

250 In the Methodist Church it has been the custom for the candidates' own minister to receive them into full membership, and at present the Chairman of the District is only occasionally invited to administer the rite, though this practice is increasing. In the Church of England confirmation has traditionally been one of the most valued pastoral functions of the bishop. When the Methodist Church becomes episcopal, how far, it may be asked, will the Methodist bishop exercise this function? Many Methodists value the custom of reception by the circuit minister, for it seems to them most fitting that the minister who has been responsible for the preparation of the candidates, and who will continue to be in close pastoral contact with them, should himself receive them. They also point out that the circuit minister directly represents the Conference, and that therefore he himself embodies an element of episcopal function.

251 While fully appreciating the reasons given for valuing presbyteral administration, it is well known that 'the Church of England, without making it a condition of intercommunion, would express the hope that the rite of confirmation, episcopally administered, would in due course come to be widely, and, in the end, generally used in the Free Church'.[1] The reasons which Anglicans would give for this hope are as follows:

[1] See *CRE*, p. 45.

252 First, in confirmation the bishop acts as father-in-God of his people, ministering spiritual things. There is always the danger that episcopacy may be channelled into administrative officialdom; this has not been an unknown tendency in the Church of England. Confirmation is an occasion when the bishop is brought into close ministerial contact with members of the Church at a moment of deep spiritual significance in their lives.

253 Secondly, the bishop, as head of the local church, representing the whole Church to the diocese and the diocese to the whole Church, seems the appropriate minister to receive candidates with prayer into full membership, both of the local and of the universal Church. At confirmation it is desirable that the vision of the wider Church should become real to the candidates, and an effective symbol of this is the presence and ministry of the bishop.

254 Thirdly, there has been throughout Christian history a continuous tradition associating the rite of confirmation with the bishop. Even in the Eastern Church, where presbyteral confirmation is the rule, this connection with the bishop has, however tenuously, been maintained through the use of oil which has been episcopally blessed. In the Roman Catholic Church, where in rare cases priests are given power to confirm, they do so only by special authority from the Pope, and the chrism used must be consecrated by the bishop. The Churches of the Anglican Communion have everywhere held to the tradition of episcopal confirmation.

255 We suggest that it would greatly help the growing together of our Churches if, while presbyteral and episcopal confirmation remain as possible alternatives within the Methodist Church, the minister conducting the service could be named in some such way as 'the bishop or some presbyter acting in his stead', according to the practice adopted by the Church of South India.

256 A further point of difference between our Churches in matters of initiation is that whereas in the Church of England confirmation is invariably accompanied by the laying on of hands, in the proposed new Methodist service the laying on of hands is optional, and the outward sign at present most generally used is the giving of the right hand of fellowship. The right hand of fellowship has significance as reception into the Spirit-filled Body of Christ. The laying on of hands is, in holy Scripture, both a natural accompaniment of prayer and also an outward sign of identification or reception and of commissioning for service (Acts 12. 3).

257 It is intended that during Stage One Methodists, who for the most part will not have been episcopally confirmed, will be welcome to receive Holy Communion in Anglican churches, though confirmation will still be required of Anglicans before they become communicants in their own church. The fear has been expressed that this procedure will appear invidious, and lend itself to abuse. The abuse feared is, however, imaginary, since the only Methodists who will be entitled to present themselves for Holy Communion in the Church of England will be those who, after due preparation, have been publicly received into full membership, or confirmed, in the Methodist Church. Such reception will raise no new problems of principle, for under certain circumstances the Church of England already welcomes to Holy Communion baptized communicants of other Churches who have not been episcopally confirmed.

258 The prospect of the ordination during Stage One of Methodist ministers who have not been episcopally confirmed has caused concern to some Anglicans. It should be pointed out, however, that the Convocations in 1955 decided that there was no objection to such a practice in the case of the Church of South India, on the ground that baptism alone, without episcopal confirmation, is a sufficient prerequisite for ordination.

12 The Churches and Marriage

Introduction

259   The 1963 Report on pp. 48–9 stated: 'There will be agreement on the part of both Churches to respect the discipline of each other's Church over its own members.... The marriage discipline of either Church would be respected by the other.' The common understanding of how this obligation of mutual respect should be honoured by both Churches is of great importance in the pastoral relations which will exist between the Churches during Stage One. The clarification of the statement quoted above has been given a high place in the list of matters which have been raised both by Convocations and by the Methodist Conference.

Common Ground

260   In their positive statements regarding the nature of Christian marriage, the Church of England and the Methodist Church do not significantly differ. The Regulations Concerning Marriage and Divorce of the Convocation of Canterbury (1957) state:

> According to God's will, declared by Our Lord, marriage is in its true principle a personal union, for better or for worse, of one man with one woman, exclusive of all others on either side, and indissoluble save by death.

The Declaration of the Methodist Church (1939) on the Christian View of Marriage and the Family states:

> In the light of the New Testament principles and teaching the Methodist Church is at one with other Christian communions in affirming as the norm and standard of Christian marriage the life-long and exclusive union of one man with one woman.

Differences

261   There is, nevertheless, a great difference in the attitude of the two Churches on questions relating to divorce and re-marriage. The current practice of the Church of England is indicated in the Regulations referred to above, which run as follows:

...re-marriage after divorce during the lifetime of a former partner always involves departure from the true principle of marriage as declared by our Lord.

...in order to maintain the principle of lifelong obligation which is inherent in every legally contracted marriage and is expressed in the plainest terms in the Marriage Service, the Church should not allow use of that Service in the case of anyone who has a former partner still living.

No public Service shall be held for those who have contracted a civil marriage after divorce.

262 The Methodist practice is laid down in Standing Order 275 of the Methodist Conference, which provides as follows:

If a request is made by any person whose previous marriage has been dissolved, whether such a person is a member of Society or not, to be married in a Methodist Church or by a Methodist Minister elsewhere, or should a civil marriage already have been contracted by any such person and a request made that a religious Service in a Methodist Church may follow such marriage, the request shall be considered by the Minister concerned after he has interviewed both parties. Every endeavour must be made to uphold the principles and ideals embodied in the Conference Statement on Divorce and the Conference Declaration on the Christian View of Marriage and the Family. Should the Minister be in any doubt as to the proper course to take, he shall refer the matter to the Ministers of the circuit, who in their turn may refer any case about which there is doubt to a special committee called together at the discretion of the Chairman of the District. In all cases the Minister shall consult the Chairman of the District before arrangements are made for the ceremony.

Pastoral Care

263 The pastoral care of those who have been divorced is a matter of great concern to both Churches, but the way in which this is exercised differs.

264 The Convocations' *Regulations Concerning Marriage and Divorce* state:

When two persons have contracted a marriage in civil law during the lifetime of a former partner of either of them, and either or both desire to be baptized or confirmed or to partake of the Holy Communion, the incumbent or other priest having the cure of their souls shall refer the case to the Bishop of the diocese, with such information as he has and such recommendations as he may desire to make.

If the Bishop is satisfied that the parties concerned are in good faith and that their receiving of the Sacrament would be for the good of their souls and ought not to be a cause of offence to the Church, he shall signify his approval thereof both to the priest and to the party or parties concerned: this approval shall be given in writing and shall be accepted as authoritative both in the particular diocese and in all other dioceses of the province.

265 In the Methodist Church, Standing Order 274 lays down the following procedure:

If any member of the Methodist Church has been a party to, or has been charged with adultery in, proceedings ending in the dissolution of marriage, the question of continuance in membership shall be considered by the minister and his colleagues in consultation with the Chairman of the District. The minister shall bring the resulting recommendation to the Leaders' Meeting for approval and implementation. If the recommendation is not approved by a majority of the Leaders' Meeting, the matter shall be referred to the District Pastoral Committee which shall in due course communicate its judgment to the Leaders' Meeting for action in accordance therewith.

Recommendations

266 We do not think that the differences of interpretation and practice which exist in our two Churches can be resolved immediately. We believe that in view of the urgent pastoral problems involved and the increasing uncertainty in secular society regarding these matters, the questions involved must be the subject of early joint consultation in our Churches. Meanwhile, as long as these differences continue to exist, it is necessary to establish clear principles of action for carrying out the pledge to respect each other's discipline.

267 Where a person who owns allegiance to the Church of England proposes, after divorce and while a former partner is still living, to marry a person (whether Anglican or not) who is outside the Methodist discipline, the decision should be clear. If such a person applies for marriage in a Methodist Church, the minister, because he is pledged to respect the discipline of the Church of England as defined in the Regulations of the Convocations, must refuse permission.

268 But where the proposed marriage is between an Anglican and a person who owns allegiance to the Methodist Church, it would not, in our opinion, be a breach of the pledge, if, after carrying out the

requirements laid down in the Methodist discipline and in consultation with his Church of England colleague, the Methodist minister agreed to solemnize the marriage.

Drawing Together

269 We do not wish to minimize the serious differences of interpretation which are implied in the differing procedures and discipline in the two Churches. At the same time, however, we recognize that these differences are not exclusive to the Church of England and the Methodist Church. Many Christian communions, Catholic, Orthodox, and Reformed, while united in a common desire to uphold our Lord's teaching on marriage, differ from one another in important points of interpretation, particularly in relation to the permissibility of divorce. We nevertheless hope that, under the guidance of the Holy Spirit, and through drawing together in our pastoral ministry, our two Churches will find a common mind on these important issues.

13 Matters for Settlement during Stage One

Introduction

270 If a marriage is to prosper, some questions about life together must be settled before the ceremony; but others, relating to the more distant future, have to be left open, since their resolution will ultimately depend on the development of the marriage relationship itself. It is important to agree which questions come in which category. Similarly, in the present negotiations, some issues confronting the Commission are of the second type rather than the first, and it is important to agree which they are. In this chapter, we take note of four such questions, each looking forward in some way to Stage Two, of which no final solution is possible in principle till Stage One is well advanced. We believe that as soon as Stage One begins a permanent Joint Commission should be set up to keep these questions, and the progress of the entire relationship, under constant review, and to advise both Churches as to what further action the developing patterns of partnership may require.

When will Union Take Place?

271 The only possible reply to this question is: 'as soon as both Churches are ready, and circumstances permit'. Entry into Stage One will be a mutual pledge to unite in one Church as soon as may be, but no time-limit can be set. The date will depend on several factors: the settling of the other questions listed below; the readiness of congregations and ministers throughout the country to cope with the domestic upheavals of merging (uniting congregations, closing buildings where necessary, accepting ministers of the other Church as pastors, etc.); the number of ministers still in service who have not accepted the Services of Reconciliation; the number of ministers and congregations remaining to whom the idea of union is still unwelcome; the possibility of other Churches taking part in the union; and, doubtless, other circumstances not foreseeable at present.

How will Ordained Ministers be Deployed in the United Church?

272   This question arises because of the sharp contrast between the Anglican system of private patronage and the 'parson's freehold', guaranteeing unlimited tenure of office, and the Methodist system of invitation by the circuit and yearly 'stationing' by the Conference. Both systems have their own strengths and weaknesses. The Anglican pattern is under discussion at present, and may soon be modified. But, in any case, joint discussions will be needed over a number of years to find the procedure which will retain the maximum of what is valuable in the two present systems, in the way best adapted for effective ministry to our complex and fast-changing contemporary society. It may well be that an arrangement is called for by which the two systems overlap each other during the process of integration.

273   Related to this is the question of what kind of episcopacy, and size and structure of dioceses, and what relation between the bishop's pastoral, administrative, and judicial functions, is to be desired in the new Church. Many Anglicans believe that some dioceses are too large to allow of a fully satisfactory pastoral ministry on the bishop's part. The position of suffragan bishops is also anomalous in a number of ways. No common mind exists as yet, however, as to what should be done. Methodist experience with episcopacy during Stage One could be of the utmost value as the two Churches together seek the 'new model episcopacy' for which the united Church of the future calls.

274   We urge that as soon as Stage One begins joint Pastoral Commissions should be set up in each area to consider the whole question of effective ministry to the people of the locality. If this led to study of the practical problems which must spring from the two Churches' differing administrative units (dioceses and districts, deaneries and circuits), and to suggestions for closer integration and assimilation in particular areas, it would be all to the good.

How will our Two Traditions of Worship be Blended in the United Church?

275   Unity does not mean uniformity, and it is inconceivable that congregations of either Church will at any stage have the forms of worship that are traditional in the other Church thrust upon them. 'Liturgical' and 'free' worship will undoubtedly coexist in the united Church. Those brought up in the one tradition will, of course, as a preparation for union, seek to learn the ways of worshipping

which are practised in the other. Thus, though forms may differ, a common approach to worship is likely to emerge, especially if some of the imaginative experiments in worship now widespread are made together in future. The experience of the Church of South India, in which 'set' and 'free' traditions of public prayer have come together, suggests that, while considerable flexibility and variation is valuable in Sunday morning or evening worship, it is desirable to adopt common forms of service for baptism and Holy Communion, confirmation or reception into full membership, marriage, and ordination. The experience of the Methodist Church points in the same direction. The work of the Joint Liturgical Group, and the direct consultations that already take place between the Liturgical Commission of the Church of England and the Faith and Order Committee of the Methodist Church, make it probable that already in Stage One a good deal of liturgical assimilation will take place.

276 It may well happen that the united Church will bring into being as the basis of its worshipping life a book of common worship. This might include (*a*) new approved forms of service; (*b*) forms of service previously used in one or other or both of the two Churches and now approved for continuing use in the united Church; and (*c*) 'directory' material, giving patterns and content for the 'free' orders of worship that have hitherto characterized Methodism. (*b*) and (*c*) would be used by ministers and congregations at their option. Such a book would garner and conserve the best in both traditions, and could do as much to establish the character and unity of the uniting Church as the Book of Common Prayer has done for the Church of England, while at the same time preserving the vital contribution to Christian worship that is made by disciplined 'free' prayer.

What will be the Basis of Faith in the United Church?

277 The 1963 Report warned of the need to 'see that the united Church is not bound too strictly by doctrinal and other such formulations which may quickly be out of date' (p. 52). The warning is wise, but must be balanced by a further warning against doctrinal laxity. Many in both Churches would say that their allegiance depends directly on what their Church stands for, and they are obviously right to insist that the united Church should publicly stand for all that either Church stood for in separation. Any further confession of faith which the new Church may need must therefore embody the substance of the existing doctrinal standards of both Churches; it may contain more than this, but it must not contain less.

89

14 Joint Training for the Ministry

The Need for United Colleges

278 Essential to the growing together of our two Churches in Stage One is the growing together of the ordained ministry in understanding and sympathy. This, indeed, is one of the chief ways in which the Churches will move together towards the unity in diversity without which Stage Two cannot be undertaken. It is of the highest importance that clergy and ministers should come to know each other, and each other's traditions and ways of thinking, at the earliest possible stage of their careers, and, as soon as this can be arranged, as students together in united theological colleges. Britain is one of the few countries influenced by the Ecumenical Movement in which joint ministerial training is not already well established; where it is well established it invariably contributes to mutual understanding and growth in unity between the Churches.

Anglican and Methodist Colleges

279 It may be asked why the Churches in this country have not already set up such united colleges. The difficulties in the way of this are greater than may at first sight appear. Many of them are administrative. In the Church of England each theological college is independent: those who wish to be ordained apply to the college of their choice, though normally they do so on the advice of their bishop.

280 In the Free Churches also, apart from Methodism, the colleges are independent. But in the Methodist Church the theological colleges are under the control of the Church as a whole. Candidates for the ministry, after approval by their circuits and districts, are selected by a committee of the Conference, and the Conference itself finally approves them and allocates them to a college.

281 It is evident that it is not easy, before Stage One, for the Anglican and Methodist systems to be integrated. Moreover, the courses taken at Anglican and Methodist colleges differ widely from each other. In the Anglican colleges the course is largely directed by the requirements of the General Ordination Examination. In the Methodist colleges some of the students take the course in theology pro-

vided by the University in their neighbourhood, or the external degree of Bachelor of Divinity in the University of London; others take a course devised in their college to meet their particular needs. Then, the traditions of worship in the colleges of the two Churches show certain important differences, and their integration in one college is a matter which requires patience and delicacy. The problems of intercommunion are at present, before Stage One, not easy to solve.

282 The Nottingham Conference of 1964 looked forward to the setting up of ecumenical ministerial training in which all the non-Roman Churches would participate. The exploration of this possibility has taken time, and has now shown that the opportunity for realizing it has not yet arrived.

Present and Future Action

283 The difficulties mentioned so far as they concern the Church of England and the Methodist Church are by no means insuperable, and the Commission expresses the strong hope that the appropriate bodies in both Churches will seek to resolve them in the near future. It is informed that the Advisory Council for the Church's Ministry of the Church of England and the Ministerial Training Committee of the Methodist Church are being invited to set up a committee for this purpose, and that the Principals of the colleges are in consultation on the matter.

284 Meanwhile much is being done to bring the ordinands of the two Churches together. A Methodist has recently been appointed to the staff of an Anglican college, and it is hoped soon to appoint an Anglican to a Methodist college. Student exchanges for short periods between pairs of colleges are frequent, and it is usual for Anglican and Methodist theological students to meet together regularly in cities and areas where there are colleges of both Churches. Lecturers are being exchanged from time to time, and there is increasing consultation between staffs on the teaching of practical theology. In several dioceses and districts Anglican priests recently ordained and Methodist probationers join together for short courses.

15 Church, Community, and State: Some Preliminary Explorations

Introduction

285　The future of the relationship between Church and State in England was among the subjects which both Churches referred to the Commission. The Methodist Conference asked specifically for a statement on 'changes in the Establishment that should be clarified before Stage One is entered'. Since, however, the question of the Establishment is already being studied by the Archbishops' Commission on Church and State, which has been charged 'to take account of current and future steps to promote greater unity between the Churches' when making its recommendations, it would not be proper, even if it were possible, for us to put forward anything more than preliminary evaluations for our Churches to consider and provisional suggestions for others to explore further.

286　Inasmuch as our two Churches will remain mutually independent throughout Stage One, it is not necessary for detailed agreement on the reform of the Establishment to be reached before Stage One starts. But, since entry into full communion will be a mutual pledge to advance to union in due course, it is reasonable that there should be, as part of the basis for accepting Stage One, some provisional agreement on ideals and objectives in terms of which detailed proposals for relations between the future united Church and the State may be worked out during Stage One itself. Both Churches may rightly regard assurance that there is no fundamental cleavage of ideals at this point as a necessary precondition of commitment to eventual union.

National Church and Establishment

287　We suggest that it is possible to make a distinction between a Church 'as by law established' and a national Church, and that this distinction will help to prevent misunderstanding on the part of both our Churches.

288　The idea of a *national* Church is of a body of Christian worshippers in a particular area, who accept it as their responsibility to minister to the national community in that area at every level of its life. Until all the Churches have come together in a closer unity there cannot be a fully national Church: the union of our two Churches must be seen as a step towards that ideal. A national Church will not merely engage in evangelism and pastoral care of individuals, but will also seek to set before the whole community the distinctive Christian dimensions of life, to fulfil to the whole community a prophetic ministry of spiritual guidance and direction, and to serve the whole community by identification with its needs, concerns, and problems, and by labouring to lead it at every point into Christian ways. Within the consciousness of a national Church is a constant tension between the sense, on the one hand, of being wholly distinct from the nation as such, as being a colony of heaven and a local outcrop of the international Church catholic, and, on the other hand, of being wholly involved with the nation, as being part of it, and charged by God to seek its good. It is the sharpness with which a Church feels this tension of involvement that shows how far it has a national character and spirit.

289 For a Church to be national in this sense, it need not regard itself and the nation as coterminous, nor need it be established. Its national character is a matter of how it understands its churchly calling, and does not depend for its reality on the status which the national community gives it.

290 What, now, is an *established* Church? It is a national Church, constitutionally recognized by the State as the Church of the nation. The State is an organ of the national community, working through processes of law and government to maintain social order and to further the common good. Establishment is a relation whereby the State officially acknowledges God in upholding his Church. The relation is a complex one, having legal, social, and cultural aspects which vary in different times and communities. In the nature of the case, the relation grows out of a nation's history, and, though it may be modified by agreement, its essential character will always be conditioned by unique features in that history; so that the present and potential significance of any particular Establishment can be grasped only through knowledge of its place in the total history of the nation during the time that this relation has existed.

291 No biblical principle forbids Establishment. The State is called to serve God no less than the Church is, and to recognize and support the Church is one natural and obvious way of doing this. From the Church's standpoint, however, there is need to watch lest the

pastoral advantages which Establishment brings should be bought at too high a price. For many English Christians, the word 'Establishment' has the unhappiest associations, suggesting social and educational privilege, political servility, spiritual lethargy, lack of liberty and integrity, and injustice both to Christians who are not of the established Church and also to citizens who make no Christian profession—injustice which sooner or later produces anti-clerical and anti-Christian reactions. These associations reflect episodes in English and European history, some of them very regrettable. It is no wonder that some have thought that established status is always an enemy of spiritual effectiveness.

292   But an Establishment based on the will of the people, and managed with due regard for the Church's self-government on the one hand, and the rights of citizens on the other, would not naturally produce any of the bitter fruits listed above, while the benefits that it could bring to the community, in terms of Christian influence and service by the Church, are clearly very great.

The Church of England

293   The Church of England is 'by law established'. Its partnership with the State is part of England's history. This partnership has never had a written basis, and does not depend on a theory, Hooker's or any other, for its existence; it is a fact belonging to the givenness of English life. At the present time, the partnership is sustained (so we judge) by an inarticulate but definite wish on the part of the community as a whole that England should remain a Christian country, with its government, law, and education resting on Christian principles.

294   Traditionally, such things as the Coronation service, the offering of prayer on parliamentary, judicial, and civic occasions, the appointment of bishops and other dignitaries by the Crown, the place of Parliament in ecclesiastical legislation, the chaplaincy system in the armed forces, prisons, and more recently hospitals, and the contributions of the Church to national education and of the state to church schools and Christian education, have manifested the reality of this historic partnership. Its dissolution would be a tragic loss, but this is not to say that it does not need reconsideration in the light of present needs.

295   The present constitutional links between the Church of England and the State are the remains of a settlement reached when

both Crown and Church were powerful political bodies in their own right. Today, however, whatever may have been true in the past, the State has no political fear of the Church, and nothing to gain from exploiting it; nor does such exploitation take place. Parliament at the present time manifests little wish to use its legislative veto to thwart any proposals on which the Church has demonstrably made up its mind, unless they would infringe existing rights of Her Majesty's subjects. The Church of England today has a great measure of ordered freedom, and the Establishment in England, unlike that in some other countries, does not involve any regular financial dependence on the State.

296 Nevertheless, the existing Establishment has its weaknesses. The benefits which it has brought, in terms of 'Christianizing' influences in national life and the attempt through the parochial system to provide pastoral care for every person in the parish, have been balanced by less happy features. Today, disabilities previously imposed on non-Anglican Christians have been largely removed, but the place of Parliament in ecclesiastical legislation, and of the Crown in ecclesiastical appointments, are widely felt to be difficulties. Methodists certainly feel this, and so do many Anglicans.

The Methodist Church

297 The Methodist Church does not think of itself as an established Church, although, in common with the other Free Churches, it enjoys full legal recognition, and shares with the Church of England in such 'invisible endowments' as exemption of its buildings from rates and taxes, paid chaplaincies in hospitals and the armed forces, grants for educational and social services, and favourable terms for the purchase of sites in new towns and development areas. But, however true it may be that the contrast between the 'Established' Church and the 'Free' Churches, as regards relations with the State, is not as sharp and clear as is sometimes thought, the Methodist Church is unambiguously self-governing in all matters of practice and policy within the limits set by the Methodist Church Union Act of 1929, and subsequent amending Acts, and Methodists expect that the future united Church will be no less clearly seen to govern itself than the Methodist Church is seen to do now.

298 At the same time, however, it must be stressed that the Methodist Church manifests a national character and spirit to a very marked degree, as witness its record of social action during the past century, the present work of its Christian Citizenship Department,

and the impressive body of social judgements contained in the volume *Declarations of Conference on Social Questions.*

299 Accordingly, we believe that in interpreting the present proposal of union as a step towards the reintegration of the broken national Church of this land, with a view to its renewal for mission and ministry to the whole of our national community, and every area of national life, we carry with us the mind and heart of both our Churches. In this understanding of the scheme, which will give direction to all that we shall undertake together during the next generation, our Churches are, as we believe, already at one. The only hesitations on this score that have appeared in either Church are as to whether the other Church feels this sense of its duty keenly enough. We believe that such anxieties are needless, and we are confident that out of this common vision regarding the task to which the united Church is called can grow full agreement in planning that relation to the State which will best aid it in fulfilling its high vocation.

Towards a Renewed National Church

300 That there is need today for a more dynamic ministry to our people than either of our Churches has achieved in isolation will not be disputed. We face growing secularism, shrinkage of congregations, and an increasingly peripheral contact between the organized Churches and the political, social, economic, and cultural substructures of present-day community life. In our plural society, where all forms of community service are attempted by the State and all group interests are catered for by their own distinct organizations, the Church appears as one of many modes whereby part of our society finds a group identity over against the rest, and is not felt to have significance for the whole nation. No doubt it is a strong temptation to accept this situation, and in it to cultivate a sect-mind and a spirit of inward-looking detachment from the pressures and problems of the larger world outside. But the temptation must be resisted. The call to our two Churches in the new era of partnership now dawning, and to the one united Church to which we look forward, is to set ourselves with new zeal to fulfil a servant-ministry to our whole society by bringing the light of God in Jesus Christ to bear on every area of thought and action in national life. The division of values between 'the gospel for the individual' and 'the gospel for society' must be transcended. The one gospel of Christ, with both its individual and its social implications, must be brought to bear on the whole community.

301　This calls for a strategy of engagement with the whole wide range of our national life, and a radical rethinking of inherited institutional patterns. At the local level, for instance, the fact must be faced that the old ideal of 'parson and parish church' serving a strictly defined territorial area is increasingly inadequate to meet actual pastoral needs. Local congregations, of course, there must be, but structures of ministry, ordained and lay, are required that can serve the needs of wider areas. Aspects of the Methodist heritage may gain a new significance at this point in the coming era. Again, ways must be sought of service in the gospel towards the complex array of humanitarian institutions in modern society—educational, medical, and social. There must be understanding and service in the realm of local government and municipal affairs. There must be a ministry of identification with, and service to, both sides of industry, together with a planned policy towards radio, television, other mass media, and the arts. The reintegrated national Church must earn its place in the community by the quality of the service which it renders as a Church and which its members render as citizens.

What Changes are Necessary?

302　During Stage One our Churches will have to consider what formal links between Church and State, what constitutional and institutional pattern of partnership, will enable the Church of the future to give best service to God and men in our secular and plural society.

303　The members of the Commission would discount two possible courses of action. First, an *establishment of ecclesiastical privilege*, such as the Church of England once enjoyed, would be as fatal in practice as it is wrong in principle. The almost complete erosion of privilege from the present Establishment is a cause, not for regret, but for profound thanksgiving by Anglicans and non-Anglicans alike: it would be disastrous to turn the clock back at this point.

304　Second, *formal disestablishment* does not appear to be a fruitful solution either. To end the historic association between Church and State by the Church's own act and request would be likely to mean loss for both sides without any compensating gain for either. Far more than formal links would perish; hard as it is now for the State to secure a Christian moral basis for national life and for the Church to resist the impulse to sectarian withdrawal, it would be harder then. Few can doubt that the present legal and constitutional ties between Church and State are of moment in the struggle for Christian truth and Christian values in an increasingly secularized community. Disestablishment was once sought by Free Churchmen to destroy Anglican privilege, and by Anglicans to secure the Church's freedom from supposed political bondage; but now we believe that the majority of both Free Churchmen and Anglicans see more clearly how desirable it is to retain a positive partnership between the Church and the State, less perhaps for the Church's sake than for the State's. And this is likely to be, not less, but more true when the united Church comes into being.

305 If the coming union (in which it must be hoped that other Churches will join) is to be a reintegration of the broken Church for the better fulfilment of its national mission, the historic Church–State relationship, modified as necessary in detail, would seem to secure to the new Church its most appropriate institutional form. This modification should be, like any other adaptation of a living relationship, as radical as is necessary and as conservative as is possible.

306 The 1963 Report declared: 'It is to be assumed that the united Church will be free to settle its own forms of doctrine, worship, and discipline, to appoint its own officers, and to settle disputes in its own courts with the same degree of freedom from State control as is now possessed by the Church of Scotland' (*Report*, p. 52). This is one side of the matter.[1] Another side of the matter is that new links with the national community must be forged. We suggest that one fruitful avenue to explore may be the strengthening of the relationship between the national Church and the Sovereign. The Crown, which has come down to us as part of the Christian heritage of the nation, maintains its historic place as a symbol and focus of national unity, and we urge that ways in which the Sovereign may be associated with the life of the united Church should be carefully explored.

307 Such suggestions can only be provisional, for they make assumptions about circumstances at Stage Two which may well be falsified by events. Also, we are conscious that issues of this kind require prolonged study and wide discussion before agreement on the wisest course can be reached, and we have no wish to anticipate or foreclose this. Our hope is that during Stage One both Churches in consultation with Crown and Parliament will make plans to secure at Stage Two (*a*) a governing body that will be truly representative and finally responsible for the doctrine, worship, and administration of

[1] The recent reform of ecclesiastical courts in the Church of England, and its present moves towards synodical government, should be understood as steps in this direction.

the Church; (*b*) a procedure whereby bishops and principal officers may be appointed by the united Church in such a way that they will be recognized by the State and nation; (*c*) a positive clarification of the relation of the Sovereign to the united Church. If, as we believe, there is substantial agreement within and between our Churches as to our common calling to serve the nation, agreement on these matters should not prove impossible to secure.

16 Legal Issues

308 The proposals for Stage One cannot be implemented without legislation. We list in this chapter the various points at which this need will, or may, arise.

An Enabling Act

309 If our two Churches accept the proposed scheme, an Act of Parliament will be necessary for the following purposes:

i. to authorize the holding of the Services of Reconciliation;

ii. to authorize the appointment of Methodist bishops and their consecration by bishops of the Church of England;

iii. to authorize the use of the proposed new Ordinal;

iv. to authorize the performance by ministers who have taken part in the Services of Reconciliation of ecclesiastical duties in the other Church;

v. to authorize performance by Anglican readers of the duties of Methodist local preachers, and vice versa;

vi. to authorize the proclamation of banns and the solemnization of marriages in Anglican churches by Methodist ministers;

vii. to authorize joint participation in services in buildings shared under the legislation referred to in paragraph 318 below.

310 At the same time, the Act must safeguard the independent status and autonomy of each Church during Stage One, and will therefore need to provide that Methodist ministers who take part in the Services of Reconciliation, or are episcopally ordained or consecrated bishops in the Methodist Church subsequent to the Services, will not thereby become liable to the provisions of the Clerical Disabilities Act, which forbids Anglican clergy to sit in the House of Commons, or of the Clerical Subscription Act, which requires of Anglican clergy an oath of allegiance and formal assent to the Thirty-nine Articles and the Book of Common Prayer.

311 A draft Bill for these purposes is appended to this chapter.

312 If this Bill became law, it would ensure that whatever a minister, or lay officiant, was entitled to do in his own Church he could also, by invitation, do in the other; but he would not thereby acquire any permanent rights, status, or exemptions in the other. This would mean, for instance, that no Methodist minister could be licensed in the Church of England, or presented to a living, without first taking the proper oaths (i.e. the Declaration of Assent, the Oath of Allegiance, and the Oath of Canonical Obedience).

Other Matters

313 *Invitation to Officiate* It is intended that a Methodist minister should be free to invite an Anglican to preach in his church without having first to obtain the consent of the incumbent in whose parish the Methodist church is, though he should be informed as a matter of courtesy.

314 It is intended also that Anglican incumbents should be free to invite Methodists to preach in their churches, but provision should be made that no Methodist minister may celebrate Holy Communion in a parish without the consent of the Parochial Church Council.

315 *Admission to Holy Communion in the Church of England* It will need to be explicitly enacted that any member of the Methodist Church may receive Holy Communion after the Services of Reconciliation in any Anglican church, notwithstanding the rubric at the end of the confirmation service in the Book of Common Prayer which declares, 'there shall none be admitted to the holy Communion, until such time as he be confirmed, or be ready and desirous to be confirmed'. The application of this rubric to Free Churchmen has been disputed, but there must be no room left for doubt as to the welcome which Methodists will receive at Anglican services of Holy Communion, and therefore a new enactment will be needed.

316 *Marriage Services in Anglican and Methodist Buildings* Section 3 (5) of the draft Enabling Bill provides for the solemnizing of marriage by Methodist ministers in Anglican buildings according to Anglican usage, and there is already nothing in law to prevent an Anglican priest from officiating in a marriage on Methodist premises, in the presence of the Registrar of Marriages or an 'authorized person' and with the authorization and consent required by sections 43 and 44 of the 1949 Marriage Act. But if it were desired to permit the solemnization of marriage in Anglican churches according to the Methodist rite, or the solemnization of marriage after banns in

Methodist churches, amendment of the Marriage Act would be needed.

317 *Church Schools* It is clearly desirable that some voluntary schools maintained by our two Churches should come under a measure of joint control during Stage One. This will raise certain points of law which will have to be considered by the appropriate bodies in both Churches. It is not possible to say precisely how these matters might be settled until discussions have been initiated with the Schools Council of the Church of England Board of Education, the National Society, the Methodist Education Committee, and the Department of Education and Science.

318 *Jointly Owned Buildings* We understand that a Bill is being promoted to permit joint ownership of church buildings.

319 *Trust and Endowments* It has been asked whether these will not need to be modified. It appears, however, that this question will arise only at Stage Two, and therefore we do not pursue it here.

ANNEXE

Draft of the Bill

320 Preamble.

DRAFT OF THE BILL TO

Make it lawful for the Church of England and the
Methodist Church to carry out their proposals for reconciliation with each other and for the sharing by each
Church in the worship and ministry of the other Church
and to provide for other matters arising in connection
with such reconciliation; to make the like provision with
respect to the reconciliation of the Church in Wales and
the Methodist Church; and for purposes connected with
the matters aforesaid.

Whereas the Church of England and the Methodist
Church have resolved, by resolutions of the Convocations
of Canterbury and York and the Church Assembly and of
the Methodist Conference, that the two Churches shall,
after many years of separation, be reconciled with a view
to their future growth together in fellowship so that in
due time they may be united:

And whereas it is proposed by the two Churches, by
resolutions of the bodies aforesaid, that their reconciliation shall be achieved—

(*a*) by holding in such places and at such times as may be
required services in a form which has been approved
by the said bodies (which form of service is hereafter
referred to as 'the Service of Reconciliation') whereby the members of each Church will be received into
the fellowship of the other Church and of its ministry;

(*b*) by the acceptance by the Methodist Church of
episcopacy in continuity with the historic episcopate
and the practice of such episcopal ordination of its
ministers for the future; and

(*c*) by the acceptance by both Churches of a common
Ordinal in a form which has been approved by the
bodies aforesaid;

and that this reconciliation shall have the effect of bringing the two Churches into full communion with each
other and securing a mutually recognized and accepted
ministry, and so enabling ministers and other members
of each Church to take part in the worship and work of
the other Church:

And whereas the Church in Wales and the Methodist

103

Church have resolved to the like effect with respect to the reconciliation of those two Churches by resolutions of the Governing Body of the Church in Wales passed in pursuance of powers conferred by Canon and resolutions of the Methodist Conference, and have approved by such resolutions the Service of Reconciliation and the said common Ordinal with such modifications as appear to the said bodies to be appropriate:

BE IT ENACTED, etc.

321 Service of Reconciliation.

1. It shall be lawful for the ministers and other members of the Church of England and the Methodist Church, notwithstanding any statutory or other legal provision, to take part in the Service of Reconciliation, and for the said Service to be held in churches of either Church or elsewhere.

322 Acceptance of Episcopacy by Methodist Church, and use of common Ordinal approved by both Churches.

2. It shall be lawful, notwithstanding any statutory or other legal provision,

(a) for the Methodist Church to accept episcopacy and episcopal ordination as mentioned in the preamble to this Act, and for the Methodist Conference to make such provision as may be necessary to give effect to this acceptance, and in particular to appoint ministers of the Methodist Church to be consecrated as bishops in that Church;

(b) for bishops in the Church of England to consecrate, or join in consecrating, as bishops in the Methodist Church (both initially and at any subsequent time) ministers of that Church appointed as aforesaid, and for the ministers to receive such consecration;

(c) for bishops and other ministers of both Churches to use the common Ordinal approved by those Churches in accordance with the preamble to this Act or any revised common Ordinal approved in like manner.

323 Sharing of ministry and worship.

3. (1) This section shall take effect as from a date announced by a notice signed jointly by the Archbishops of Canterbury and York and the President and Secretary of the Methodist Conference and published in the London Gazette as the date on which the two Churches are to be regarded as entering into full communion with each other.

(2) On and after the said date, notwithstanding any statutory or other legal provision,

(a) ministers of each Church who have taken part in the Service of Reconciliation or have been ordained after the said date may, by licence or invitation, conduct or share in conducting worship in churches or other buildings of the other Church, and such worship may be in accordance with the forms of service and practice of either Church;

(b) such ministers as aforesaid of each Church may, for the purpose of assisting the ministry of the other Church at times of need, conduct or share in conducting worship in churches and buildings of their own Church in accordance with the forms of service and practice of the other Church (but without the presence of a minister of the other Church);

(c) such ministers as aforesaid of each Church may administer the Holy Communion to members of the other Church, who may receive it;

(d) in the case of forms of service which, according to the practice of the Church whose forms they are, may be conducted in whole or in part by a reader or preacher (not being a minister), the foregoing provisions of this section shall apply to any such reader or preacher of either Church, as respects such forms of service or parts thereof, as they apply to such ministers as aforesaid;

(e) where in accordance with the foregoing provisions of this section worship is conducted in accordance with a form of service and practice of the Methodist Church, in a church or other building of the Church of England, that worship may on that occasion take the place of a service which a minister of the Church of England is required by law to conduct there.

(3) Where a church or other building is shared by the two Churches under any enactment relating to the sharing of churches, the agreement or trust for sharing the church or building may make such provision for the participation of the ministers and members of each Church in the ministry and worship of the other Church as may be appropriate having regard to the foregoing provisions of this section.

(4) In the application of this section to the service of Holy Communion, 'minister' means a minister who according to the doctrine or practice of his Church may conduct that service.

(5) For the purposes of the Marriage Act 1949, in relation to the publication of banns and solemnization of marriages in a church or other building of the Church of England or used by that Church under any enactment relating to the sharing of churches, the expression 'clergyman' shall include a Methodist minister who has taken part in the Service of Reconciliation or has been ordained after the date appointed under this section, and the reference to Holy Orders in section 25 of the said Act shall be construed in like manner; but save as aforesaid nothing in this section shall affect the requirements of the said Act.

324 Independent status of the two Churches.

4. It is hereby declared for the avoidance of doubt that:

(a) no Methodist minister shall by reason only of any one or more of the following, that is to say—
   (i) his taking part in the Service of Reconciliation,
   (ii) his episcopal ordination as a Methodist minister,
   (iii) his consecration as a bishop in the Methodist Church by a bishop of the Church of England or by a Methodist bishop,
   (iv) any provision of section 3 of this Act,
   be subject to the jurisdiction of any bishop of the Church of England (including his jurisdiction as ordinary) or of any ecclesiastical court, or to any disqualification or disability as respects any secular office or appointment or any secular activity;

(b) no minister of the Church of England shall by reason only of his taking part in the Service of Reconciliation or any provision of section 3 of this Act be subject to the jurisdiction of the Methodist Conference;

(c) no minister or member of either Church shall by reason only of his taking part in the Service of Reconciliation or of the mutual reception of members of the two Churches provided for in that Service be subject to the jurisdiction of any officer or authority of the other Church or be qualified for appointment or election to any office in the other Church for which a special qualification is prescribed by any statutory or other legal provision;

(d) no minister or other member of either Church shall by reason only of any one or more of the matters mentioned in paragraph (a), (b), or (c) of this section be subject to any statutory or other legal provision binding on ministers or other members of the other Church as respects doctrine, discipline, or forms of worship (including uniformity of worship);

(e) the Clerical Subscription Act 1865 shall not apply in relation to the Service of Reconciliation, the episcopal ordination of a Methodist minister, or the appointment of a Methodist minister to any office in the Methodist Church; and

(f) the rights of Her Majesty in respect of appointments to any offices in the Church of England shall not be taken as applicable to offices in the Methodist Church.

325 Application to Methodist Church of Overseas and Other Clergy (Ministry and Ordination) Measure 1967.

5. Section 1 of the Overseas and Other Clergy (Ministry and Ordination) Measure 1967 (which enables an overseas clergyman as defined in the said Measure to officiate as priest or deacon in the province of Canterbury or York and to obtain ecclesiastical preferment) shall apply to Methodist ministers who have taken part in the Service of Reconciliation or have been ordained after the date mentioned in section 3 hereof, as it applies to overseas clergymen, and section 4 of the said Measure (which provides for the performance of episcopal functions by overseas bishops as so defined in any diocese in either such province) shall apply to Methodist bishops as it applies to overseas bishops:

Provided that section 1 (6) and section 4 (3) of the said Measure (which relates to ecclesiastical offences) shall not apply to Methodist ministers and bishops.

326 Subsequent entry into the reconciled ministries.

6. Where any ministers of either Church do not take part in the Service of Reconciliation on or before the date mentioned in section 3 hereof, it shall be lawful, notwithstanding any statutory or other legal provision, for a service to the like effect, and in a form approved by the Convocations of Canterbury and York and the Church Assembly and by the Methodist Conference, to be held in churches or other buildings of either Church or elsewhere, and for such ministers to take part therein and for all other requisite persons to conduct, or participate in the conduct of, that service, and thereupon the provisions of this Act shall have effect in relation to such ministers in all respects as if they had taken part in the Service of Reconciliation and as if the service to the like effect were the Service of Reconciliation.

7. (1) The foregoing provisions of this Act shall, so far as applicable, apply for the purpose of carrying into effect the reconciliation of the Church in Wales and the Methodist Church, subject to the following modifications:

(a) for the references to the Church of England there shall be substituted references to the Church in Wales;

(b) the references in section 1 to the Service of Reconciliation and in section 2 to the common Ordinal shall be construed as references to the Service and Ordinal as approved by the Church in Wales and the Methodist Church in accordance with the preamble to this Act;

(c) the date on which under section 3 (1) the two Churches are to be regarded as entering into full communion with each other shall be a date announced by a notice signed jointly by the Archbishop of Wales and the President and Secretary of the Methodist Conference and published in the London Gazette;

(d) for the reference in section 6 to a service in a form approved as therein mentioned there shall be substituted a reference to a service in a form approved by the Governing Body of the Church in Wales and the Methodist Conference.

(2) For the purposes of this Act, both in its application under this section and otherwise, any provision applicable to ministers and other persons who have taken part in or are affected by the Service of Reconciliation or a service to the like effect shall apply to all such ministers and persons irrespective of whether the Service concerned was held by the Church of England and the Methodist Church or by the Church in Wales and the Methodist Church.

8. (1) In this Act except where the context otherwise requires

'statutory or other legal provision' means any Act or Measure, any instrument or document made or having effect under or by virtue of any Act or Measure, any trust instrument or other instrument or document of any nature whatsoever, or any rule of law, being an Act, Measure, instrument, document, or rule in force at the passing of this Act;

'the Methodist Church' means the Methodist Church in Great Britain, and 'Methodist' shall be construed accordingly.

(2) References in this Act to the taking part by a minister of either Church in the Service of Reconciliation, or in a service to the like effect, are references to such participation therein as involves the reception of that minister by that service into the fellowship of the ministry in the other Church.

329 Short title.

9. This Act may be cited as the Anglican–Methodist Reconciliation Act 19 .

Notes on the Draft Bill by Sir Harold Kent

330 *Preamble* The preamble recites resolutions of the central bodies of the Church of England and the Methodist Church, assumed to have been passed before the introduction of the Bill, setting out—

(*a*) the resolve of the two Churches to be reconciled with each other,
(*b*) the means by which the reconciliation is to be achieved, and
(*c*) the effect which it is to have.

The advantage of this recital is, first, that it makes clear that the reconciliation springs from the decisions of the two Churches and derives its spiritual authority from those decisions, and that the purpose of the Parliamentary Bill is to give legal effect, so far as necessary, to those decisions. Secondly, the recital takes out of the enacting part of the Bill questions as to whether the steps proposed are valid and sufficient from the theological point of view, and will have the intended effect. These questions probably cannot be wholly excluded from debate in Parliament, but they will be presented as matters already decided by the two Churches and not as matters to be decided by Parliament.

The form of the Bill has some analogy with that of an Act giving effect to an international treaty. The treaty is recited by the Act or scheduled to it, but cannot be amended, and the purpose and scope of the Act is limited to making such changes in the domestic law as may be necessary to give legal effect to the treaty.

331 *Clause 1* This clause makes it lawful for ministers and other members of the Church of England and the Methodist Church to take part in the Service of Reconciliation 'notwithstanding any statutory or other legal provision'. This phrase recurs in other clauses and is defined very widely in clause 8 to include Acts and Measures, subordinate legislation, trust deeds and other instruments, and legal rules, that may stand in the way of the reconciliation and its intended consequences. On the Church of England side the main difficulties arise out of the Acts of Uniformity, the Book of Common Prayer including the Ordinal, the Clerical Subscription Act 1865, and the law relating to the consecration of churches. The main difficulties on the Methodist side arise out of the doctrinal standards laid down by clause 30 of the Deed of Union, which cannot be amended or overridden except by Parliament (see the provisos to section 8 (2) of the Methodist Church Union Act 1929 and to the second recital to the Deed of Union), and the trust deeds on which Methodist churches are held.

332 *Clause 2* This clause removes any legal impediment, arising from the doctrinal standards mentioned above, to the acceptance by the Methodist Church of episcopacy in continuity with the historic episcopate (see the preamble) and the episcopal ordination of Methodist ministers. It also provides for the appointment of Methodist bishops by the Methodist Conference, which might otherwise be regarded as infringing the Crown prerogative to appoint bishops. Paragraph (*b*) of the clause allows Anglican bishops to consecrate or join in consecrating Methodist bishops and for the latter to receive such consecration, matters which might otherwise offend against the doctrinal law of their Churches, and paragraph (*c*) authorizes the use by both Churches of the common Ordinal referred to in the preamble. The latter provision is needed for the Church of England because, although an alternative Ordinal could be authorized under the Prayer Book (Alternative and Other Services) Measure 1965, that authorization could only be of a temporary and experimental character.

333 *Clause 3* This clause provides in subsection (1) for the date of entry of the two Churches into full communion with each other, which is to be announced by a notice jointly signed by the Archbishops of Canterbury and York and the President and Secretary of the Methodist Conference. Subsection (2) spells out the various ways in which each Church may, 'notwithstanding any statutory or other legal provision', share in the ministry and worship of the other Church.

Subsection (3) looks forward to the passing of a Bill for the sharing of church buildings, now under active consideration, and enables the sharing agreement or trust to provide for the matters set out in subsection (2). The latter subsection would not apply as it stands, because it is drafted in terms of separate buildings.

Subsection (5) enables a Methodist minister to conduct an Anglican marriage service in a church of the Church of England. It is not necessary to make the converse provision, because Part III of the Marriage Act 1949 would allow a minister of the Church of England, with the necessary authorization and consent, to conduct a Methodist marriage in a Methodist church.

334 *Clause 4* This clause is in the declaratory form 'for the avoidance of doubt', and its main purpose is to make it clear that the two Churches are to remain independent entities, subject to their own rules and disciplinary systems and not to those of the other Church. Other matters provided for are that—

(a) Methodist ministers are not to be subject to secular disabilities attaching to Anglican ministers, such as disqualification for membership of Parliament;

(b) a minister of either Church is not to become eligible by reason only of his taking part in the Service of Reconciliation for ecclesiastical office in the other Church (but see the note on the next clause);

(c) the Clerical Subscription Act 1865 is not to apply to the Service of Reconciliation or to Methodist ordinations and appointments;

(d) Crown rights of appointment to bishoprics and other dignities in the Church of England are not to apply to Methodist offices.

335 *Clause 5* This clause applies the recent Overseas and Other Clergy (Ordination and Ministry) Measure 1967 to Methodist ministers who have taken part in the Service of Reconciliation or have been ordained after the date announced under section 3. The effect is to enable such ministers, with the written permission of the Archbishop of Canterbury or York, as the case may be, to officiate or obtain ecclesiastical preferment in either province as if he had been ordained by a bishop of that province.

336 *Clause 6* This clause enables ministers of both Churches who do not take part in the original Service of Reconciliation to take part in a subsequent service 'to the like effect' approved by the two Churches, and so to come within the provisions of the Bill. The clause has no application to ministers ordained after the date announced under clause 3 to whom the Bill will apply automatically.

337 *Clause 7* The terms of this clause have been settled with advisers of the Church in Wales. It envisages a separate reconciliation between that Church and the Methodist Church, and accordingly subsection (1) applies the earlier provisions of the Bill for that purpose, with appropriate modifications. The words 'so far as applicable' exclude provisions which have no application to the Church in Wales, e.g. clause 4 (e) and clause 5.

Subsection (2) deals with the problem of ministers who go from one country to the other. This problem obviously affects Methodist ministers, because there is no separate Methodist Church in Wales, but it is not uncommon for ministers in the Church of England or the Church in Wales to take ecclesiastical office in the other Church. The effect of subsection (2) is that the Bill is to apply both in England and Wales to all ministers who have taken part in the Service of Reconciliation, irrespective of whether the Service was one held by the Church of England and the Methodist Church or the Church in Wales and the Methodist Church.

338   *Clause 8*   Reference has already been made to the definition of the phrase 'statutory or other legal provision'. It would no doubt be possible to have a more specific list, but the only result would be to give rise to legal argument, and the definition is in fact limited by the contexts in which it is used to matters relevant to the Bill.

The other provisions of this clause require no comment.

339   *Clause 9*   The alternative title would be one setting out the three Churches concerned, which would be rather long and clumsy and would become impossible if the Bill were extended to the Episcopal Church in Scotland.

The clause contains no provision as to the extent of the Bill. This is in fact limited by the Churches to which it applies, and it is thought that a territorial limitation would be out of place. For example, a minister of the Church of England who happened to be staying in Scotland ought to be able to take part in a service in a Methodist church on the same basis as in England. This question may, however, require further consideration, as also the question of application to the Channel Islands and to the Isle of Man.

17 The Position in Wales

340 The situation in Wales is, in many respects, more complicated than it is in England.

The Methodist Church and the Church in Wales

341 The Methodist Church consists of an English section and a Welsh section.

The English-speaking circuits in South Wales (with over 18,000 members) are formed into the Cardiff and Swansea District, whilst those in North Wales (with nearly 6,000 members) form part of the Chester and Stoke-on-Trent District. There are also a few circuits in Mid-Wales (with about 1,000 members) belonging to the Birmingham and the Wolverhampton and Shrewsbury Districts. All these circuits are served by ministers who are regarded as being in 'the English work', very few of whom are bilingual. They usually serve in Wales for a period of time and then return to circuits in England.

There are 101 active ministers and 58 supernumerary ministers in the English work.

342 The Welsh-speaking circuits are grouped into three Districts, the First North Wales, the Second North Wales, and the South Wales, with an aggregate membership of over 14,000. Four Welsh circuits attached to the First North Wales District are wholly or partly in England. There is also one Welsh circuit in London, which forms part of the London N.E. District. The ministers who serve these circuits are regarded as being in 'the Welsh work' and usually spend their whole ministry in Welsh-speaking circuits, although it is possible for them to be transferred to 'the English work'.

There are 63 active ministers and 21 supernumerary ministers in the Welsh work. Five ministers live in England.

In most of these circuits the language is Welsh, but a few use only English, and individual churches in others use English either regularly or occasionally, to meet the needs of an ever-changing situation.

343 In the Church in Wales the difference in language is not reflected in corresponding division in structure, and the Methodist division between English and Welsh congregations is foreign to it. Therefore, in the coming together of the two Churches, geography and language constitute a problem that will have to be solved, and we commend to the Churches the careful study of it which is contained in *Anglican–Methodist Union in Wales* (pp. 59–75).[1]

344 Despite the division into English and Welsh Districts, every Methodist District in Wales (as in England) forms part of the Methodist Church in Great Britain, and is governed by the decisions of the Methodist Conference. The Church in Wales, on the other hand, is an independent province of the Anglican Communion, with its own Governing Body.

Towards Action in Wales

345 In such a momentous development in ecumenical relations as is envisaged in this Report, it is highly desirable that the Church in Wales should move at the same time as the Church of England, if that is at all possible. Indeed, the anomaly would be so great as to be almost intolerable if the Church of England were to be in full communion with the Methodist Church, whilst the Church in Wales was not. It would be an equally serious anomaly if the English Districts in Wales were in full communion with the Church in Wales and the Welsh Districts were not. The only satisfactory procedure would be for the Church of England and the Church in Wales to enter simultaneously into full communion with the Methodist Church, both English-speaking and Welsh-speaking.

346 To meet this situation two steps have been taken:

(*a*) The Church in Wales and the Methodist Church in Wales have been represented on the Commission.

(*b*) A parallel body was set up in Wales in 1965—the Anglican–Methodist (Wales) Negotiating Committee.

The main documents of the Commission have been made available to the Welsh Committee, and its comments and observations have been carefully considered by the Commission.

The Negotiating Committee has published a Welsh version of *TR*, *Tuag at Gymod*, and intends in due course to publish its own Report.

[1] *Anglican–Methodist Union in Wales* (Church in Wales Publications, 1965).

We trust that it will be able to approve of the Commission's Final Report and to commend it to the Churches in Wales.

347 The Constitution of the Church in Wales requires that 'any proposal concerning faith, discipline, or ceremonial, or concerning any article, doctrinal statement, rites, ceremonies, or formularies of the Church in Wales' shall be introduced and enacted by Bill procedure in the Governing Body. This procedure takes at least two years. The Commission hopes that all necessary steps can be taken to ensure that the Church in Wales can enter upon Stage One at approximately the same time as the Church of England. The Legal Panel of the Welsh Negotiating Committee works in consultation with the Commission's Legal Working Party, and the draft Parliamentary Bill (paragraphs 320–9 above) has been so framed as to cover Wales as well as England.

348 The Welsh Negotiating Committee keeps under review the whole ecumenical scene, and tries to relate its own specific task to the larger one of bringing all God's people in Wales into a visible unity.

18 The Position in Scotland

349 The Ecumenical Movement has stirred Christians in Scotland, as elsewhere, to a deep concern about church relations. If this is to prosper, however, the particular circumstances of existing relationships must be understood and respected. The Commission recognizes that national history and tradition have a valid place in the life of Churches and that, therefore, what is suggested for England may not be directly applicable to Scotland. There is need for Christians in England to appreciate the different situation north of the border; and, equally, for those in Scotland to understand, and if possible to support, the recommendations for England, even if they cannot take comparable action themselves.

Methodism and the Episcopal Church in Scotland

The situation may be described as follows:

350 Methodism has an historic link with the Church of England, but not with the Church of Scotland nor with the Episcopal Church in Scotland; yet Methodism in Scotland has always valued its close relationships with the national Presbyterian Church, by which it has been much influenced.

351 In England Methodism forms a considerable part of Free Church life and witness, but on the mainland of Scotland it is one of the smallest denominations, in little contact with any of them apart from the Church of Scotland. The same is largely true in the Shetlands, where Methodism is relatively somewhat stronger.

352 In contrast with these other denominations Methodism has a vital link with England, for its churches are fully integrated parts of the Methodist Church of Great Britain, sharing equally in decisions to be made for England. The great majority of Methodist ministers appointed to Scotland are English and expect to serve again in England. Their people, however, have a close affinity with Presbyterians and will not support changes which seem to them to injure this relationship.

353 The Episcopal Church in Scotland, though quite separate from the Church of Scotland, is also distinct from the Church of England,

being an independent member of the Anglican Communion, not bound by the decisions of the Church of England but making its own decisions within Scotland, and claiming an historic link with the Christian Church in Scotland from earliest times. Nevertheless, it is bound to be concerned about its relationship with Methodism in Scotland as a consequence of reconciliation in England. The Episcopal Church and Scottish Methodism have had very little contact in the past; both are now engaged in separate conversations with the national Church.

Possible Courses of Action

354 In view of these facts the Commission has asked itself if the recommendations for England could be reproduced in Scotland, especially as the Episcopal Church welcomed the proposals of the 1963 Report, finding them generally acceptable, and would be prepared to consider proceeding to Stage One in Scotland, subject to its being satisfied with the treatment of various matters dealt with in the present Report. This could mean the holding of a Service of Reconciliation in Scotland, and the consecration of a Methodist bishop, or bishops, for Scotland. We are convinced that, if possible, reconciliation should take place where the ministers concerned are serving and with the participation of their people, and it is for this reason that we would welcome a development along the lines just indicated.

355 We recognize, however, that, because of the close links of Methodists with Presbyterians, the appointment of a Methodist bishop for Scotland is unlikely to be acceptable to Methodists at the present time. That this is so has been made plain by resolutions of the Scotland and Zetland Synods, expressing their reaction to *TR*. If this is a final judgement, due weight must be given to this fact. But it must also be remembered that Methodist ministers serving in England could be appointed to Scotland after having shared in the Services of Reconciliation, and ministers now serving in Scotland could be appointed to England. We recommend, therefore, that, if it is found to be inadvisable to proceed to an act of reconciliation in Scotland and to the consecration of a Methodist bishop for Scotland, those ministers in Scotland who desire to share in a local Service of Reconciliation at the inception of the scheme should be invited to do so at a Service somewhere in England. The Methodist Conference should ensure episcopal oversight for its ministers so participating, though continuing the present office of Chairman, appointing as such a minister other than a Methodist bishop.

356 In the meantime, the movement towards church union should be encouraged by the assurance of the Methodist Conference to Methodists in Scotland that any move which led to their union with the Church of Scotland, if desired by them, would be warmly supported. In the event of Scottish Methodism taking an incomplete share in Stage One, its relationship with the Episcopal Church in Scotland would need to be adjusted accordingly, appropriate arrangements being made in regard to individual Methodist ministers who had personally accepted the scheme and taken part in a Service of Reconciliation.

19 The Way of Reconciliation

The Services of Reconciliation: Their Aims

357 It was proposed in the 1963 scheme that Stage One (full communion between our two Churches) should be inaugurated by a liturgical Service of Reconciliation. The Commission revised the 1963 text of this Service for its Interim Statement (*TR*), and has revised it further for the present Report. It now appears in two forms, the first for central, the second for subsequent local, use. In both forms it shows by its Declaration of Intention and its structure that its aim is threefold.

358 First, it announces before God and men the pledged purpose of our two Churches to become one. The first words of the Declaration of Intention are: 'We are met together in the presence of God, in obedience to his call, to lay before him the resolve of our two Churches to unite in one Church.' From this standpoint, the Service is an act of *commitment*.

359 Second, it brings to an end the long period during which our two Churches have existed in mutual independence. This is achieved by the reception of the total membership of each into the fellowship of the other, and into a shared responsibility for all that enters into that mission to the world to which each Church believes itself to be called. From this standpoint, the Service is an act of *reconciliation*; hence its name.

360 Third, it brings together the ordained ministries of our two Churches in a way designed to make each fully acceptable to all members of the other, with the prospect of each ministry being henceforth fully acceptable also to all Churches with which either the Church of England or the Methodist Church is in full communion at present. This is achieved by the laying on of hands with prayer upon every minister of each Church by a chief minister of the other. The basis for this prayer is stated as follows: 'We wish now to share each in the spiritual heritage of the other'; 'We offer ourselves wholly to thee, asking that thou wilt renew in us thy blessings already given, and that thou wilt transcend the differences of our calling and make us one by bestowing upon us what thou knowest us to need for thy

service as (bishops) (presbyters) in thy universal Church and in the coming together of the Church of England and the Methodist Church.' What is asked for in the prayer is that each minister will be so blessed by God that all the divine gifts and qualities which are present in ministers of the other Church may henceforth be given to him, together with any further enrichment that he may need for service in the new relationship of reconciliation. From this standpoint, the Service is an act of *integration.*

361 The Service of Reconciliation has been a subject of sustained controversy in both our Churches since 1963. It has been criticized as being both offensive in principle and likely to prove ineffective or harmful in practice, and some ministers of each Church have declared that they cannot in good conscience take part in it. Since the intention of the Service will largely be frustrated if insufficient ministers are ready to take part, and since it is a prime concern of the Commission that the scheme should not have divisive and embittering effects in either Church, it is desirable to discuss this matter fully, and in the light of all the varied objections and difficulties that have come to our notice. This is the reason for the extended treatment that follows, which we hope that both our Churches will study with special care.

Visible Unity and Ministry: The Problem

362 The problem of integrating the ministries of our two Churches —the problem which the Service is designed to solve—is created by the following three facts:

ONE

363 'The visible unity of the Church', according to the Lambeth Appeal to All Christian People of 1920, 'will be found to involve the wholehearted acceptance of the Holy Scriptures...the Creed commonly called Nicene...the divinely instituted sacraments of Baptism and the Holy Communion...and a ministry acknowledged by every part of the Church as possessing not only the inward call of the Spirit but also the commission of Christ and the authority of the whole Body.' The Appeal continues: 'May we not reasonably claim that the Episcopate is the one means of providing such a ministry?' Consistently since 1920 the Church of England, in common with other Anglican Churches throughout the world, has adhered to this 'Lambeth Quadrilateral' as containing the four necessities for full communion with itself. It is clear that, though many Anglicans see the fourth point as a matter of post-apostolic order, and therefore as

standing on a different footing from the first three, which belong to the realm of faith, yet almost all regard it as a proper part of the Anglican platform, their reasons including, on the one hand, the practice of the greater part of the Christian Church from early times in which they see the divine guidance and, on the other, the belief that, as the Lambeth Appeal affirmed, only an episcopal ministry can hope ever to be acknowledged by every part of the Church.

364 The requirement of an episcopal ministry has been written into the constitution of all Anglican Churches, as witness some further words of Lambeth 1920: 'In accordance with the principle of Church order set forth in the Preface to the Ordinal of the Book of Common Prayer, [the Conference] cannot approve the celebration in Anglican churches of Holy Communion for members of the Anglican Church by ministers who have not been episcopally ordained.' In England, of course, such celebrations would be illegal. Whether Anglicans may properly receive Holy Communion at non-episcopal Eucharists, and whether under any circumstances the requirement of an episcopally ordained celebrant for Anglican Eucharists might be relaxed, are questions on which members of the Church of England divide.

TWO

365 The Methodist Church wholeheartedly accepts the holy Scriptures, the Nicene Creed, and the sacraments of Baptism and Holy Communion. But the ministry of the Methodist Church has not been commissioned by, or integrated with, the historic episcopate. Yet Methodists hold that the establishing by their Church of a non-episcopal ministry was fully justified, and it is common ground that the Methodist Church should not, and in practice could not, be asked to repudiate or cast doubt upon the ministry of word and sacraments in the Church of God which it believes was bestowed on its ministers at their ordination.

366 The Lambeth Appeal declared: 'It is not that we call in question for a moment the spiritual reality of the ministries of those Communions which do not possess the episcopate'; and this acknowledgment, which the Church of England has consistently maintained since 1920, has been axiomatic throughout the present conversations. It is reiterated in the integration of the ministries in the revised Services of Reconciliation. However, the fact remains that at present Methodist ministers may not lawfully celebrate Holy Communion in English parish churches.

THREE

367 The Lambeth Appeal of 1920 laid it down that 'for all the truly equitable approach to union is by the way of mutual deference to one another's consciences'. How can Methodist ministers satisfy existing requirements for ministry in the Church of England without violence being done to any Methodist consciences? Alternatively, how can Methodist ministers be enabled to celebrate the Holy Communion in Anglican churches without giving offence to any Anglican consciences? It is these problems which the ministerial part of the Services of Reconciliation seeks to resolve.

Revision of the Service of Reconciliation

368 The Service of Reconciliation has been further revised in the light of the many comments received. The Commission recognizes the force of the criticisms that the earlier versions were too much concerned with looking backwards and too clerical in character. The form now proposed, therefore, places a much greater emphasis on the reconciliation of the Churches and upon the mission to which they are called. The renewal of the Covenant has been brought into that part of the Service which is the joint act of both Churches and in it reference is now made to the hope of wider unity: 'We should all pledge ourselves to pray and to work for closer unity between our Churches and with all other Christian people.' The integration of the ministries follows on, and is more definitely subordinated to, the reconciliation of the Churches and more clearly follows from it.

369 The ministerial part of the reconciliation has been reshaped to take account of the following points:

(a) The publication of the revised Ordinal with its statement on the Ministry which becomes the determinative document for the intention of the two Churches in respect of the ministry.

(b) The fact, not made sufficiently plain in the two previous versions, that the integration of ministries is between a threefold ministry on the one hand and a single ministry on the other, with the consequence that there cannot be exact parallelism in the treatment of each.

(c) The wish of many that the consecration of the first Methodist bishops be more clearly incorporated in the act of reconciliation.

370 It is now proposed that the reconciliation of the Churches and the integration of the ministries be effected by three successive Services, possibly spread over a week. These are as follows:

371 *The central Service of Reconciliation* conducted by the President of the Methodist Conference and the Archbishop of Canterbury. Its main feature is the reconciliation of the Churches and their pledge to seek organic unity, but it also includes the reception of the Anglican episcopate by the Methodist Church and the reception by the Church of England of those Methodist ministers who are to preside at the local Services, followed by a commissioning of them and of the bishops who are to act with them for this purpose.

372 *The local Services* on the days following the central Service. They provide an opportunity for the members of the Churches, throughout the country, to join in the reconciliation, and for the integration of the priests of the Church of England and the ministers of the Methodist Church. Each will be conducted by a bishop of the Church of England and a Methodist minister (referred to in the Service as the Presiding Minister) commissioned at the central Service to do so.

373 *The consecration of the first Methodist bishops* which might take place on the Sunday following the central Service of Reconciliation.

374 The deacons of the Church of England (that part of the three-fold ministry not provided for separately in these acts) will be reconciled along with the rest of the Church, but will be brought into the unified ministry as they are subsequently ordained presbyter according to the new Ordinal.

375 The ministerial Declaration to be made before the Services has been retained, but its wording has been simplified to make it more clearly forward-looking, and provision is also made for those who though now ministers of the Church of England or the Methodist Church were originally ordained in some other Church from which they have transferred. A correspondent has drawn our attention to the unsuitability of the earlier form for this situation.

376 A number of ceremonial directions which appeared in the earlier versions have now been omitted. We recognize that if our Churches accept this way of reconciliation, it will be necessary to set up a committee to work out the many practical details involved, and we think it best to leave a number of these ceremonial points to that committee's decision. It will also be for our Churches then to decide which liturgy for the Holy Communion shall then be used, but in printing the present version we have found it convenient to set

out most prayers in the form in which they appear in the 1662 Communion Service which is common to both Methodists and Anglicans.

The Acts of Reconciliation: Their Contents

377   The Service of Reconciliation was designed, as has been said, to bring together for unity and mission, by a public liturgical action, two Churches whose people and ministers have long been separated from each other, have often been in competition and conflict with each other, and are still divided from each other in many places by ignorance, suspicion, and indifference. This is still the primary and comprehensive purpose of the acts of reconciliation. As part of this purpose, they seek to provide each Church with a ministry which will be fully accepted by the other and, so far as this can be secured, by every other part of the Church; and to do this in a way which does not require members of either Church to repudiate or question in any way the ministry which they believe its ministers to possess and exercise.

378   Both the central and local Services of Reconciliation follow the same broad pattern. Within the first part of the Communion Service, the Liturgy of the Word, is set the reconciliation of the Churches. The central Service may be regarded as the public sealing of the resolutions passed by the governing bodies of the two Churches. The local Services carry this throughout the length and breadth of the country.

379   This reconciliation contains six elements:

First, a declaration of intention, which includes the reading of the resolutions of the two Churches authorizing their coming together.

Second, an act of penitence for the sinfulness that has been in their division and the hindrances to the gospel caused thereby.

Third, an act of thanksgiving for God's gifts in the past, to which is added a brief intercession for the Church, its unity and mission.

Fourth, the renewal of the Covenant. Here a prominent feature of Methodist devotion is used for the purpose of a new dedication of the two Churches to God and as a means whereby they pledge themselves to work for closer unity with each other and with all other Christian people.

Fifth, this renewal of the Covenant is followed by brief, representative acts of reception into fellowship of the whole membership of either Church by the other, ending in the greeting and handclasp of their two principal ministers.

Sixth, the two Churches, now reconciled, join in a common confession of faith and thanksgiving.

380 These six elements are divided up by the collects, scripture readings, and psalmody of the liturgy. The Old Testament lesson speaks of God's promise of renewal, the Epistle of the unity of our faith and calling and of the diversity of gifts bestowed by Christ upon his Church. The Gospel reminds us that the example set by the Lord is one of service.

381 The reconciliation is followed by the integration of the ministries, begun in the central Service, continued in the local Services, and concluded in the consecration of the first Methodist bishops. In order to avoid unnecessary complication and lengthening of the Services the Anglican bishops, but no priests, will be integrated at the central Service, and priests, but no bishops, at the local Services. It is possible that the numbers of bishops involved may make it desirable to hold the central Service in two parts, one in the North and the other in the South of England. Alternatively, only those bishops who are to preside at the local Services should take part in the central Service and the integration of the rest be incorporated in the service for the consecration of the first Methodist bishops. These are matters which may be left to a decision nearer the time by the committee referred to earlier in this chapter.

382 The integration of the ministries makes important use of the new Ordinal and its statement on the ministry, which set out the common belief and intention of the two Churches for the ministry in their coming together. The integration is designed to bring about a unity between those who have been ordained according to the differing rites of either Church before the reconciliation and those who will be ordained thereafter under the provisions of the new Ordinal. In the prayers God is asked to bestow the grace and gifts needful for this purpose, and in order to emphasize this the greater part of each prayer said over the ministers of either Church consists of a portion of the appropriate prayer from the new Ordinal, preceded by a petition for the sending of the Holy Spirit in the context of the coming together of the two Churches.

An Unambiguous Intention

383 A distinction must be drawn between the intention with which those participating will come to the Service and any opinion or belief that they may have about what is happening in it. All will believe that what may conveniently be called an enlargement of commission is being bestowed. Some will believe that the grace of ordination is given also, others that it is not, and many will perhaps be agnostic on this point. The prayers are so worded as to leave the determination of that issue in God's hand: we pray that the Holy Spirit may be sent upon 'each according to his need'. But the intention of the rite is not in doubt. It is to secure that every minister taking part shall receive whatever he may lack of the gifts and grace bestowed upon the ministers of the other Church, and that all shall come together as fellow-presbyters according to the pattern and doctrine of the ministry agreed by the two Churches. This intention is stated in three places: first, in the Declaration subscribed by each participating minister before the Services of Reconciliation begin; second, in the statement read at the start of the integration of the ministries; and third, in the prayer following that statement which is recited jointly by all the participating ministers.

384 The intention is clear and definite, but it does not foreclose the theological issue (still debated in the Church of Rome as elsewhere) between those who hold that the normative character of episcopal ordination admits of no exception, and those who believe that circumstances may justify or necessitate ordination in other ways than by bishops.[1]

[1] Cf. *IS*, p. 27.

20 Theological Objections

385 Various objections have been made to the ministerial part of the Services of Reconciliation, from different points of view. It is desirable to examine these, in order to assess the adequacy of the rationale given above.

386 They fall into two classes. Some are theological, reflecting doubt as to whether acceptance of the Services is consistent with regard for, and obedience to, God's truth. Others are practical, reflecting doubt as to whether use of the Services will in reality advance the purpose of growth into union, and not rather obstruct it. An attempt will now be made to state the major objections in their strongest form, and to meet them in terms of the position so far set out.

The first class of objections includes the following:

The Services are a subterfuge, because of their deliberate ambiguity on the crucial issue of ordination

387 'The Services decline to say whether the laying on of episcopal hands on Methodist ministers is intended to confer ordination or not, and instead devise a form of words which can be taken either way. But this is theologically frivolous. Moreover, the claim that the Services are an act of reconciliation is made empty while licensed disagreement stands at its heart, and the criticism that the scheme is insufficiently concerned for unity in faith and truth becomes unanswerable.'

388 The deliberate ambiguity is admitted; the defence of it is that, in view of the wide extent of doctrinal agreement already established, no theological obligation to clarify this issue before, or in, the Services remains. The doctrinal statements produced in the course of these conversations since 1958 have made it clear that existing differences on the question of whether or not Methodist ministers lack a 'character' or commission which only episcopal ordination can bestow do not affect either our common recognition that the Methodist ministry has been owned and used by God, or our common understanding of the gospel of free grace. But issues which, whatever their

importance, do not touch the fundamentals of the gospel of free grace may be safely left for unhurried exploration in future theological debate. To say this is simply to apply the principle of historic Anglican comprehensiveness to the matter in hand. If it is not held to have been frivolous on the part of the Church of England to allow its members freedom to interpret its own Ordinal in opposed ways, according to their conscientious convictions on this question, then Services of Reconciliation which deliberately respect and embody this measure of theological freedom cannot be thought frivolous either; nor can they be censured as a subterfuge, when the limits of this freedom, and the reasons for it, are made explicit in advance. Willingness to respect this freedom, and to receive each other on the basis of it, so far from being a hindrance to the reconciliation to which the scheme invites our Churches, is actually one element in it. What is sought is the reconciliation of Christians who, on the basis of other agreements already spelled out, are ready to allow each other freedom at this point, as Anglicans have long been doing already.

The mutual laying on of hands is superfluous, since both bodies of ministers are ordained already

389 'Since Anglican priests and bishops, and Methodist ministers, have all been ordained to the ministry of Word and Sacraments in the Church of God according to the rites of their Churches, and since the two ministries, as such, are actually reconciled in and by the reconciling of the two Churches whose ministers they are, all that is necessary or appropriate in the ministerial part of the Services is that they should recognize each other, perhaps by giving each other "the right hand of fellowship". The mutual laying on of hands is neither necessary nor appropriate. The ministerial part of the Services should be rewritten in the light of the above facts.'

390 To this it may be replied:

(i) It was shown above that the Services are needed for the public reconciliation of our two separated Churches, and also that the proposed laying on of hands with prayer is for the purpose of committing both ministries to God, that he may grant each to share in whatever gifts the Spirit has conferred upon the other. In the context of such a prayer, the laying on of hands is not in itself inappropriate.

(ii) One purpose of the Services is to regularize the relation of the two ministries to each other by incorporating the one-order Methodist ministry into the second order of the historic threefold ministry as found in the Church of England, and the priests and bishops of the

Church of England into the historic order of the Methodist ministry. The laying on of hands with prayer by a minister who has authority in his own Church to ordain is an appropriate sign of this aspect of integration.

(iii) The fact must be faced that, while many Anglicans accept the ordination of Methodist ministers without reservation, others believe that Methodist ministers will not be truly ordained without the laying on of hands with prayer by a bishop in the historic succession, and there are yet others who, while they do not categorically deny the ordination of Methodist ministers, entertain doubts and scruples regarding any ministry that has not been formally integrated with the historic episcopate and presbyterate. Were the laying on of hands omitted from the Services, many Anglicans would be excluded by their convictions from the fullness of reconciliation into which the two Churches wish to enter.

The Services are improper, because they are a concealed ordination of Methodist ministers

391 'Since the Services of Reconciliation contain all the elements required for ordination according to catholic tradition, they must be regarded as in reality an episcopal ordination of those Methodist ministers who take part, even though this is not explicitly said to be their intention, and they are given a different name. But in that case Methodist ministers, who believe themselves to be ordained in the Church of God already, cannot with a good conscience participate.'

392 Undoubtedly those who believe themselves to be ordained already cannot without contradiction believe that they will be ordained again to the same office in the Services of Reconciliation. A minister's ordination is once for all, and in this sense reordination is not so much improper as impossible. Therefore the Services, which admittedly can be interpreted as conveying episcopal ordination to Methodist ministers if one's theology requires that interpretation, are suspected by some of being an irreverent mockery, as if by taking part they would be condoning and acting a lie. There is in reality no mockery and no lie. Any Anglicans who wish to believe that Methodist ministers are being ordained in the Services will know that the Methodists themselves, and many Anglicans also, deny this to be so, and they will have accepted this knowledge in advance. All in either Church who think that ordination is not involved will know that some Anglican participants believe otherwise, and this knowledge

also will have been accepted in advance. Thus there is no trace of dishonesty, hypocrisy, or pretence, but only an accepted difference of opinion, such as can be frequently found among Christians of different schools of thought who come together for the administration and reception of the Sacraments of the gospel.

393 It should be noted, however, that nothing in the Services themselves demands the view that it is an ordination of those who have not been episcopally ordained. No minister, Methodist or Anglican, will take part until he has subscribed a declaration testifying that, though he comes to the Service in a spirit of receptiveness, yet he comes to it as a minister already ordained in the Church of God. It should be noted too that all the elements required for the ordination of a minister according to Methodist tradition are found in the laying on of hands with prayer upon the Anglican clergy. If it is not felt necessary to object that this part of the rite is a concealed presbyteral ordination for Anglicans, then it should not be felt necessary to treat the laying on of hands on Methodists as an attempt to ordain them episcopally; and those who do not argue that Anglicans should abstain, on the grounds that the Services involve a concealed ordination of them, cannot consistently argue that Methodists ought to abstain on this account.

394 In fact, the avowed intention of the ministerial part of the Services, as was shown, is to offer both ministries to God and to each other, praying that whatever God has given to either he will henceforth give to both. Such an intention transcends the conflict of opinion which this objection reflects.

The Services are improper, because the law will interpret them as an episcopal ordination of Methodist ministers

395 'It is legal opinion that when a bishop in the historic succession lays his hands on Methodist ministers using the prayers prescribed in the Services of Reconciliation, those ministers will become, in English law, episcopally ordained. None, therefore, will be able to deny that the Services of Reconciliation have conferred episcopal ordination upon Methodist ministers. Conversely, if the law decided otherwise, it would be necessary to affirm that the Services had not conveyed episcopal ordination. The point is that the law will decide, one way or the other, and this rules out liberty of interpretation and frustrates the professed intention to defer to Methodist consciences by leaving open the question whether the Services involve episcopal ordination or not. The law will resolve this question, even if the

Churches decline to do so. This is intolerable in itself, and the verdict which the law is likely to give is doubly intolerable for those Methodists who can accept the Services only if liberty to deny their character as ordination is safeguarded to them.'

396 A study of the draft Bill which this Report proposes for inaugurating Stage One (pp. 103-9) will show that this objection is groundless. So far from inviting or permitting the legal verdict which the objection anticipates, the Bill makes such a verdict impossible. What the Bill, if accepted, will do is to establish the principle that the law regards Methodist ministers who have taken part in the Services of Reconciliation *as if* they were episcopally ordained priests. But nowhere will it affirm or imply that in the Services of Reconciliation these ministers actually received episcopal ordination. That question it studiously leaves open, as do the Services themselves. What is more, by establishing the principle that these ministers' rights in parish churches are *as if* they had been episcopally ordained, the Bill will create a situation in which, so far as can be foreseen, no legislation or legal ruling that decides the question whether they have been episcopally ordained or not is ever likely to be needed.

The Services cannot achieve their intended object, because they do not require Methodist ministers to intend to receive ordination as priests

397 'Methodist ministers who take part in the Services believing themselves to be already ordained to the Christian ministry in its fullness will lack the intention of being ordained as priests. Many Catholic Anglicans, who believe that Methodist ministers lack the grace of catholic ordination, do not believe that this grace will be conveyed in the Services of Reconciliation to those who lack all intention to receive it. For lack of requiring this intention, the Services will at this point be futile and ineffective.'

398 But the Church of England has never required of its own candidates for the presbyterate adherence to the particular view of priesthood which this criticism presupposes, nor has it ever treated any ordination as invalid because the candidate lacked an intention based upon this view. It would be wrong in principle to require of Methodist ministers a theological intention which goes beyond any requirement made of Anglican ordinands. In fact, the historic catholic practice, as continued in the Church of England, is and always was to regard the 'matter' and 'form' of ordination as sufficient to render the rite valid. In this case, Methodist ministers will

intend to enter, so far as may be, into 'a ministry acknowledged by every part of the Church as possessing not only the inward call of the Spirit but also the commission of Christ and the authority of the whole Body'. It is this intention which each participating minister will spell out when he subscribes the declaration that in the Service he submits himself 'wholly to God, to receive from him such further grace, commission, and authority as he may now wish to give me'. Such an intention is both perfectly appropriate in itself and, by all historic principles of catholic judgement, entirely sufficient.

The Services are anti-catholic, since they assume and require agnosticism as to the adequacy of catholic episcopal ordination

399 'By requiring a mutual laying on of hands with prayer as a condition of full communion, the Services deny full recognition not only to Methodist but also to Anglican orders. By obliging Anglican bishops and priests, as well as Methodist ministers, to declare an intention of seeking from God "such further grace, commission, and authority, as he may now wish to give me", the Services require of Anglican clergy a doctrinal agnosticism as to (i) the nature of their own priesthood and of the Methodist ministry, (ii) the necessity of episcopal ordination for the exercise of ministerial priesthood, and (iii) the adequacy of their present orders without supplemental commissioning. Such agnosticism ought not to be asked for, and cannot be professed by Anglican clergy who have clear convictions on these matters.'

400 The solution of these difficulties lies in maintaining a clear distinction between *ordination* and *jurisdiction*. The Services of Reconciliation will certainly, whatever else they bestow, initiate an extension of jurisdiction for ministers of both Churches.

401 The declaration of intention to seek such grace and authority as God may wish to give will naturally be explained in terms of the new and partly unknown demands which will be made on each minister by reason of the extended jurisdiction, and growth together of the two Churches within full communion, which the Services will initiate. The mutual laying on of hands with prayer will also naturally be explained in terms of a threefold purpose connected with this same extension of jurisdiction and purpose of growth together: (i) to be a visible sign of the Churches' common request that the Spirit of God may bestow on each minister such gifts as he needs for the new relationship; (ii) to indicate that both Churches are offering their ministries to God to receive from him mutual reconciliation, corporate

renewal, and common possession of all that the other ministry has hitherto been given during the time of separation; (iii) to give to each ministry the further explicit commission that it needs for the fulfilment of the larger task which now falls to it. This threefold purpose expresses the common ground on which the mutual laying on of hands rests; but none of this is concerned with the adequacy or otherwise of any participant's orders. The Services leave that question open, as has been said.

The Services are anti-evangelical, since they make the laying of episcopal hands on Methodist ministers a necessary condition of full communion between themselves and Anglicans

402 'To demand an episcopal commissioning of Methodist ministers as a condition of full communion is as wrong as was the demand, condemned in Paul's Epistle to the Galatians, that Gentile Christians must receive circumcision before Jewish Christians could have full fellowship with them. In each case, the demand casts doubt on a man's fitness for unrestricted fellowship with the other group, and implies that the rite is essential to establishing this fitness. To take part in the Service would imply that one accepted this estimate of the laying on of episcopal hands, i.e. that it implies an adverse judgement on the present Methodist ministry; and therefore those who, in the name of the freedom of divine grace and the sufficiency of Scripture, reject this view, cannot conscientiously participate.'

403 It has already been said that one reason why this laying on of hands has been proposed is to make it possible for Anglicans of different schools of thought to enter into full communion with their Methodist brothers. Without it, many would be excluded, and this fact, quite apart from other considerations, makes the rite desirable. But it has also been said that though individual Anglicans are free, if they wish, to regard the Services as episcopal ordination, and to believe that the nature and efficacy of a Methodist minister's sacramental acts will change when episcopal hands have been laid on him, neither Church is committed to these opinions nor to any adverse judgements on either ministry. With regard to both ministries (let it be said again), the declared intention of the Services is simply to ask God that whatever gifts either now has, or will need for the new era of partnership, may henceforth be the common possession of both.

404 But does not the fact that Anglican reception of Methodist ministers into full communion depends on their taking part in the Services speak louder than words on this point? No. The Services

will form part of a sequence of procedures which must be judged as a whole. So judged, the sequence does not naturally suggest an adverse view of non-episcopal ministries, any more than the Services' own wording does. Two facts in particular make it clear that no such adverse opinion is implied. First, individual Anglicans who wish to receive Holy Communion from the hands of Methodist ministers are not at present debarred from doing so, and it is not proposed to debar them from receiving it from the hands of non-participant Methodist ministers after the Services of Reconciliation. Second, the interpretation of the Services must be held to be governed by the firm intention, to which both Churches are asked to commit themselves, that in the united Church of Stage Two ways shall be found of maintaining the full communion with non-episcopal Churches the world over which the Methodist Church now enjoys. The Services should not be viewed apart from this commitment, which in effect is a deliberate refusal to brand non-episcopal ministries as inferior. Thus the alleged parallel with Galatians, which turns on the contention that an adverse judgement is implied by the procedure that is required, falls to the ground.

405 The argument from Paul's letter to the Galatians is sometimes developed in another way. Paul, it is said, condemns as legalistic any humanly prescribed addition to faith as a condition of full enjoyment of the Christian salvation; but the proposed laying on of hands upon Methodist ministers is precisely such an addition.

406 To this, however, there is a twofold reply. First, Paul's opponents in Galatia required not only circumcision of Gentiles, in addition to faith and baptism, but also acceptance of the doctrine that their circumcision was necessary for their salvation. This, at any rate, is the position Paul argues against, and it is *this doctrine* that he condemns as legalistic and contrary to the gospel. The fact that he himself circumcised Timothy (Acts 16. 3) shows that his objection was only to this doctrine, not to circumcision in itself. By parity of reasoning, therefore, the laying on of hands should not be thought objectionable, since there is no doctrine of its necessity for salvation which has been attached to it by either Church. Second, the stated aim of the Services is to reconcile two Churches, and to do all that is needed in our present situation to bring all members and ministers of both (who are assumed to be enjoying saving grace already) into full communion with a good conscience. This aim takes the Services right out of the realm of the Galatians debate.

21 Practical Objections

407 A second class of objections takes its rise from reflection on the probable consequences of proceeding with the Services, and expresses doubts, not so much about its soundness in principle as about its expediency in practice in our present situation. The main objections under this head are the following:

The Services will impede growth into deeper unity

408 'Whatever may be said to justify the Services in theory, in practice it is certain that a relationship based on licensed theological opposition at the professed point of reconciliation will sooner or later turn sour. There is no hope here for growth in mutual trust; what is likely to ensue, rather, is suspicion and bitterness, and the sense of being in a false position because of the way in which the cracks of doctrinal disagreement have been papered over.'

409 No doubt it is all too possible, granted the weakness of human nature, that the new relationship of Stage One might turn sour; but if it does, it will be from lack of commitment to each other, and to the long-term quest for fullness of unity, not because of the Services of Reconciliation as such. To wait until there is no such risk would be to wait for ever. Our doctrinal disagreements about the ministry are matters of stubborn fact, and no procedural device can eliminate them. They are publicly admitted, they are notorious, and there is no intention or possibility of concealing them. The proposal is that, on the basis of what we hold in common, our two Churches should advance through full communion into union, taking these present differences with us, and pledging ourselves to continue discussion together until we reach a common mind. The Commission has already declared that the act of taking part in the Services of Reconciliation, which of set purpose prejudices none of the variant viewpoints, should itself be understood as such a pledge, and has recorded its belief that if this 'intention of the Service is responsibly accepted, we may expect that under God our common thinking on this subject, during the period of full communion, and later on in the united Church, will be theologically fruitful' (*TR*, p. 15). The same responsible acceptance of this intention would be needed whatever means were taken to inaugurate Stage One, and without such acceptance the

new relationship will turn sour however it is initiated. Participation in the Services of Reconciliation is meant to signify that the difficulty of accepting each other before our differences are resolved has already been consciously surmounted, not that it has not yet been faced.

The Services will cause needless division

410 'Many ministers in both Churches have already said that they cannot in good conscience join in the Services of Reconciliation. Thus the Services will split both ministries, and bring about only partial intercommunion, not full communion, between the two Churches. Non-participating ministers, feeling themselves handicapped for conscience' sake because the terms of service in their Church have been changed over their heads, will be isolated and discouraged. Thus the Services will be discredited, and appear in retrospect an ecumenical failure. It will thus be morally impossible to recommend such a procedure again, when negotiating union with any other non-episcopal body; and if this method will have to be abandoned later on, surely it would be wiser, more straightforward, and less troublesome, to decide against adopting it now.'

411 It is unthinkable that either Church will go forward with the Services unless it is conscious of overwhelming support, and each Church will need to make careful inquiry as to whether such support is forthcoming. When such inquiry is made, those who take part in it and those who record their views will do so in the full knowledge that the total rejection of the scheme of union is likely to have permanently damaging, perhaps disastrous, effects on both Churches. There is no doubt that if, nevertheless, large numbers seem likely to withhold support, it will not be wise or right to go forward in this way. In no case, however, would either Church wish to handicap its non-participating ministers, and we are confident that, if the Services are accepted, all members of their ministries, even those who feel unable to take part in them, will play their part in furthering growth towards union in every way their conscience allows. Thus it is by no means evident that the Services will be discredited, even if some ministers remain non-participants.

412 It should in any case be added that acceptance of the Services of Reconciliation now will not commit either Church to proposing such a method of advance into union in negotiations with any other Church. The Services are not intended to establish a norm of procedure. What seems right in one situation will not necessarily seem right in another. In all future negotiations, the best procedure will

have to be determined each time on the merits of the case, and no precedent can be decisive. The question before our two Churches is not whether the Services of Reconciliation would be the right way for others in the future, but whether it is the right way *for us now*.

413 Finally, it must be said that it is unfruitful to argue that the Services of Reconciliation should be abandoned because they will divide, unless *either* one goes on to advocate no action at all *or* one can point to an alternative that will be less divisive. It is clear, however, that God is calling us to present action, and equally it is doubtful whether any alternative can be found that will command wider assent than the Services of Reconciliation. Reasons for this judgement are given in the next chapter.

The Services will make Stage One interminable

414 'The Services initiate full communion between our two Churches on the basis of an episcopal commissioning of Methodist ministers. The Methodist Church requires that all its present relations of eucharistic fellowship with non-episcopal Churches the world over should be carried into the united Church of Stage Two. If the Church of England were asked now to accept the principle of full communion with non-episcopal Churches and their ministers, it seems certain that it would be unable to agree to do so. Is it any more likely to be able to do so at any time in the foreseeable future? If not, what prospect is there of Stage Two ever being reached? Methodist acceptance of the principle of an episcopal commissioning for all ministers may enable Stage One to begin, but how can it be responsibly begun without a definite assurance that Anglican retreat from this principle will in due course enable it to end? For without such an assurance there is no reason to think that Stage One can ever end.'

415 In the nature of the case, it is not possible to give final reassurance on this point, because the future is God's, not ours, and we cannot foresee what events may bring forth, or what convictions men will have, in years to come. It is possible only to express the belief that if our two Churches establish full communion in the way that respects consciences on both sides most fully, and if at the same time they deliberately decline to prejudice future discussion by trying to foresee how the Methodist requirement will be met, they will thereby create the most hopeful conditions that our situation allows for solving this problem at a later date. The fact that part of the basis for the proposed united episcopal Churches of Nigeria, Ghana, North India, Lanka, and East Africa is an intention to maintain full com-

munion with all Churches to which any of the uniting Churches, Anglican or non-episcopal, were so related before, encourages the hope that this problem can be resolved in England too. Nor have we any right to abandon the hope that other non-episcopal Churches will reach the point of intercommunion with the Church of England before Stage One has run a long course.

At or before Stage Two the Services of Reconciliation will have to be given up

416 'The present plan involves that any Anglican or Methodist minister (from overseas, say) who wishes to enter into the fellowship of full communion between our two Churches in Stage One must first be commissioned by an appropriate minister of the other Church using the appropriate part of the Services of Reconciliation. But if at Stage Two the present Methodist principle of full communion with ministers of non-episcopal Churches as they are is accepted, or if prior to Stage Two intercommunion is established between the Church of England and a non-episcopal Church on the basis simply of a pledge to unite (something that has already happened in some Anglican provinces), then presumably this requirement will be abandoned; and how can it be right to commit oneself now to a practice which one expects to give up in due course as no longer necessary?'

417 The answer to this question is simply that different procedures are necessary at different times and in different circumstances. It must be said again that the present proposals do not seek to establish precedents, and the question whether the Services of Reconciliation are right for our two Churches now must be considered on its merits, without being prejudiced by our guesses as to what the future may require. Just as there will be no discredit in committing ourselves to the Services now, if present circumstances make this seem right, so there will be no discredit in abandoning them if future circumstances so direct. In each case the move will be, not a retreat, nor therefore an embarrassment, but a step forward, so far as Anglicans and Methodists are concerned. The Services of Reconciliation to be held at the inauguration of Stage One will take place virtually once for all; the number of those for whom they may be required in the future is comparatively small.

22 Alternatives

418 The way of integrating the two ministries by means of the Services of Reconciliation is proposed in the belief that it is the best means of doing this, for the inauguration of Stage One, that our situation allows. The two foregoing chapters have tried to answer doctrinal and practical objections to them that have been raised. But it is clear that many people suspect that, if we looked, we could find some other ways of integrating the ministries which would secure the same ends with greater effectiveness and fewer disadvantages. It is desirable at this point to review the alternative possibilities, in order to see whether this is so.

The main alternatives appear to be the following:

To establish full communion between the two Churches through mutual ordination of their ministries

419 It is suggested that each minister should submit to the form of ordination that is usual in the other Church. But this idea would certainly not be welcomed by very many in either Church. As the 1965 Convocation Report said: 'It would not be acceptable to many Methodists who would regard it as calling in question the reality of their ministry and requiring them to repudiate their spiritual history (see *Report of the Conversations*, p. 25). It would not be acceptable to many Anglicans who would regard it as implying that their own orders were in some way incomplete.'[1] The proposal could be defended only in terms of the theory that in a divided Christendom all orders have incomplete validity or authority, and so need to be supplemented from each other, but this theory is not widely held today. It may be said with certainty that if some ordained ministers are likely to decline to take part in a Service of Reconciliation, far more would decline to go through the form of being ordained again. The whole Methodist ministry, to a man, might so decline, and the greater part of the Anglican ministry too. The Services of Reconciliation, which deal with both ministries as ordained, are clearly preferable to mutual ordination, which does not.

[1] *R*, p. 17.

To establish full communion by receiving each minister into the other Church in the way that is done at present when ministers transfer

420 It is suggested that each Church should do to the ministers of the other what it would do if they were transferring to its ministry as individuals; that is, the Methodist Church should receive Anglican clergy as they are, and the Church of England should confer episcopal ordination upon Methodist ministers.

421 But the reconciling of the two Churches, with their ministries, and the establishing of full communion thereby, is quite a different thing from the receiving of individual ministers out of the one Church into the other, and there is no obvious reason why the procedure followed in the latter case should be thought best for the former. The difference between integrating the two ministries in a context of churchly reconciliation, and adding to the one from the other in a context of churchly separation, should rather be marked by the use of a *different* procedure. In any case, the likelihood of massive objection by Methodist ministers to undergoing a further form of ordination to their present office remains.

To establish full communion between the two Churches by mutual conditional ordination of their ministries

422 The purpose of conditional ordination is to remove doubts as to whether a person is ordained or not. This suggestion appears intolerably artificial, since Methodists have no doubts as to the reality of Anglican orders. The Methodist Church would not consent to the frivolity of conditionally ordaining Anglicans merely to maintain an appearance of reciprocity.

To establish a rule of receiving into full communion with the Church of England those Methodist ministers who had been episcopally consecrated or ordained

423 It is suggested that the initial act of reconciliation should consist of two parts only: a solemn pledge to unite as soon as may be, and the consecration of the first Methodist bishops. From then on, all Anglican clergy should be eligible to celebrate the Holy Communion in the Methodist Church, and those Methodist ministers who had been episcopally consecrated or ordained (the Methodist bishops, and those whom year by year they ordained) should be eligible to

celebrate Holy Communion in the Church of England. This would at first be a relation of only partial communion between the two Churches, but it would grow into full communion over half a century or so.

424 This suggestion was looked at in the 1958 Interim Statement. It was there pointed out that during the period in which the Methodist ministry was growing into full communion with the Church of England 'it would be the senior ministers in each circuit who would be placed in an anomalous position'; junior ministers, having been episcopally ordained, would stand in a relation to the Church of England which their seniors did not share. Reflection on the practical implications of this led to the conclusion that such a scheme 'would prove unacceptable to the Methodist Church in this country' (p. 40). Nothing has happened within the Methodist Church to cause a revision of this judgement.

425 Were it proposed to replace the Services of Reconciliation by this alternative, in order to avoid division for conscience' sake within our two ministries, it would have to be pointed out that the change would bring divisions of its own as well as other inconveniences.

426 First, to replace the immediate prospect of full or near-full communion by that of limited partial communion would be felt in both Churches as a grave setback, particularly discouraging for Methodist ministers now looking forward to full communion with the Church of England.

427 Second, this procedure would be slow. It would commit both Churches to a Stage One relationship which could hardly last less than fifty years, unless some further Anglican recognition of Methodist ministers were subsequently introduced, and no such step is foreseeable at present.

428 Third, the anomalous status in which the senior Methodist ministers would be involved for this length of time would be felt by the whole Methodist Church to be scarcely tolerable. It would create a deep difference of status and esteem within a ministry which is traditionally a close-knit brotherhood, and would lead to bitterness in the minds of many lay people who greatly prize the equality of respect accorded at present to all their ministers. This remains true even if the estimate is correct that in Stage One the occasions when a Methodist minister will be asked to celebrate Holy Communion in an Anglican Church will be comparatively infrequent.

429   Fourth, this procedure is more rigorous than the way now proposed, for it demands unconditional episcopal ordination as a requirement for full communion in the case of ministers. Thus it would not make it easier to honour at Stage Two the requirement that present Methodist relations of full communion with non-episcopal Churches be maintained, and could make it harder.

To establish full communion between the two Churches on the basis of mutual recognition of their ministries just as they are

430   It is suggested that, in the light of the Methodist acceptance of the historic episcopate, and of a rule of episcopal ordination, and in the light also of the solemn undertaking to unite which both Churches will give in inaugurating Stage One, each Church should enter into immediate full communion with the other, irrespective of the fact that Methodist ministers lack episcopal orders.[1] This would require legislation to permit Methodist ministers, as clergy of an episcopal Church, though not themselves episcopally ordained, to celebrate Holy Communion in the Church of England. With this, the right of individuals and congregations not to be obliged to receive Holy Communion from Methodist ministers would have to be safeguarded, since it is known that some have conscientious objections to doing this. However, the anomaly of different practices among Anglicans at this point would be progressively eliminated as more and more Methodist ministers were episcopally ordained.

431   This procedure, it may be argued, would eliminate the problems of conscience which the Service has raised for some ministers in both Churches. It would also lay a foundation for eventually resolving the problem of maintaining at Stage Two present Methodist relations of fellowship with non-episcopal Christendom. It would not prejudice the goal of organic union, and it would be likely to make any future negotiations with other Free Churches a great deal simpler. Since it may be that Methodist ministers will not often be asked to celebrate Holy Communion in the Church of England, it is contended that the practical problems and tensions which would arise would not be insuperably great. It is also argued that to bring our varying convictions and principles of action into the open in this way, and to learn to exercise Christian forbearance towards one another as each follows his conscience within the new relationship, would be a salutary discipline for both Churches at the present time.

[1] This would be an adaptation to the present two-stage scheme of the procedure by which a united ministry was secured when the Church of South India came into being in 1947.

432 But this course of action, while reducing some problems, would raise others. The very proposal would certainly bring serious division within the Church of England. The majority in both Churches might well regard the presence of ministers who have not taken part in the Services of Reconciliation as a lesser anomaly than the widespread diversities of practice to which this alternative would give rise. Its practical difficulties are likely to exceed those attaching to the present proposals, and the prospect of embarrassment for Methodist ministers in particular would be increased. It is probable that many Anglican priests would in practice refuse the recognition of Methodist ministers which had been officially agreed upon. Most serious of all, there is good evidence to suggest that the Methodist Church would refuse to accept the dislocation which would be involved in taking episcopacy into its system, if it knew that the immediate result would be something which fell so far short of full communion.

433 Also, action of this kind would raise problems in the relations of the Church of England with other episcopal Churches, both within and outside the Anglican Communion, and the Church of England could not contemplate such a move till it had assured itself that these relations of fellowship would not be endangered—an assurance which might prove hard to come by.

434 It has been suggested that, if either the fourth or fifth of the above alternatives were adopted, Methodist ministers who had not been episcopally ordained might welcome the opportunity to undergo voluntary conditional ordination by a bishop, and so render their ministry acceptable to all Anglicans without exception. In favour of this it could be said that it would not of itself involve any principle of action which is not already involved in submission by a Methodist minister to the laying on of hands with prayer in the Services of Reconciliation: for one purpose of those Services is to remove any Anglican doubts that may exist regarding Methodist orders, and the purpose of receiving conditional ordination would be exactly the same. In neither case would the person submitting to the rite naturally or necessarily imply by his action that he shared these doubts.

435 Yet Methodist ministers would certainly regard conditional ordination as less acceptable than the Services of Reconciliation; for in the latter the laying on of hands with prayer has many purposes in addition to that of removing Anglican doubts, and is related primarily to the future responsibilities that all ministers of both Churches will derive from the new degree of fellowship into which the Churches are

entering, whereas in conditional ordination the action would be related only to these doubts, and would refer solely to the past. The Methodist Church would undoubtedly hold that a Service, every part of which can be explained and justified as appropriate without reference to adverse judgements on the past, is preferable to a rite which cannot be explained or justified save in terms of such a reference.

436 The arguments here stated lead to the conclusion that the Services of Reconciliation, as now proposed, are satisfactory in terms of principle, and will bring more advantages in practice than any alternative.

23 The Acts of Reconciliation

437 (*a*)

IN these Services the two Churches, acknowledging God's call to union, place themselves before him in humility and hope. They join together in thanksgiving for his grace given to them in time past, and in penitence for failure to use his gifts aright and for all that has been of human wickedness in their divisions. Within the setting of the Holy Communion, ordained 'for the continual remembrance of the sacrifice of the death of Christ, and of the benefits which we receive thereby',[1] they seek reconciliation with each other. They pray that God will effectively bring the Members and Ministers of both Churches into full communion: they ask him to give new power to their common proclamation of the Gospel: and they pledge themselves to move forward to unity in one Church.

(*b*) The Church of England values the historical continuity of the visible Church in faith, sacrament, witness, and devotion from apostolic times. It has been accustomed, since the foundation of the Church in these islands, to seek God's grace and authority for its Bishops, Priests, and Deacons through prayer with the laying on of the hands of Bishops. It believes that this tradition has come down from New Testament times and that it is God's will that it should continue. All this the Church of England desires to share with the Methodist Church, and at the same time to enter into that Church's spiritual heritage.

(*c*) Methodists believe that within the One, Holy, Catholic, and Apostolic Church their communion was brought into being by the Holy Spirit to be a witness to the universal grace of God, to the gift of assurance by the Holy Spirit, and to the power of the Holy Spirit to make us perfect in love.[2] They desire to share with their brethren of the Church of England the spiritual tradition, order, and patterns of fellowship which, under God's guidance, this calling has brought forth, and to enter into the spiritual heritage and continuity of commission which the Church of England so greatly values.

---

[1] Catechism from the Book of Common Prayer.
[2] Methodist Senior Catechism.

(*d*) Each Bishop, Priest, and Minister taking part in the Services shall previously subscribe the following declaration, and books containing their signatures to it shall be laid on the Holy Table at the points indicated on pages 157 and 172.

THE DECLARATION

I, A.B., having been ordained to the ministry of the Word and Sacraments in the Church of God according to the rites of the Church of England,[1] Methodist Church,[1] submit myself in this Service wholly to God, to receive from him such grace and authority as he may wish to give me for my ministry as a *Presbyter*[2] in his Church in the coming together of the Methodist Church and the Church of England.

(*e*) It would be impracticable to arrange that every Member of either Church should take part in a Service of Reconciliation and for that reason the Laity present at any one Service are regarded as representative of their Church. From within the congregation at each Service two smaller groups shall be chosen to perform the acts assigned to the Laity on pages 155 and 170 of this Report.

(*f*) The Central Service will be conducted by the Archbishop of Canterbury and the President of the Methodist Conference, certain parts being taken by the Archbishop of York. Each local Service will be conducted by a Bishop of the Church of England, acting under the authority of that Church, and by a Minister appointed for the purpose by the Methodist Conference, who is referred to in the Service as the Presiding Minister. Arrangements for similar Services in Scotland and Wales will be for decision by the respective church authorities in those countries, the present Report being primarily concerned with England.

(*g*) The appropriate section of the Service relating to the Ministry shall be used separately in the case of any Minister of either Church who has not taken part in a Service of Reconciliation at the time of the inauguration of Stage One and desires at some later date to enter into the full Communion which will then exist between the two Churches.

[1] Those who have been ordained in some other Church will substitute the name of that Church and add:

and now serving in the ministry of the Church of England / Methodist Church.

[2] Bishops will substitute *Bishop* for *Presbyter*.

I

THE CENTRAL SERVICE OF
RECONCILIATION

438 (a) *The following hymn shall be sung:*

1 All people that on earth do dwell,
    Sing to the Lord with cheerful voice;
    Him serve with mirth, his praise forth tell;
    Come ye before him and rejoice.

2 The Lord, ye know, is God indeed;
    Without our aid he did us make:
    We are his folk, he doth us feed;
    And for his sheep he doth us take.

3 O enter then his gates with praise;
    Approach with joy his courts unto;
    Praise, laud, and bless his name always,
    For it is seemly so to do.

4 For why? The Lord our God is good;
    His mercy is for ever sure;
    His truth at all times firmly stood,
    And shall from age to age endure.

5 To Father, Son, and Holy Ghost,
    The God whom heaven and earth adore,
    From men and from the angel-host
    Be praise and glory evermore. Amen.

(Tune: Old Hundredth.)

DECLARATION OF INTENTION

(b) *Then shall the President of the Methodist Conference say,*

WE ARE met together in the presence of God, in obedience to his call, to lay before him the resolve of our two Churches to unite in one Church. We do so in thankfulness for his abundant blessings to us, and in penitence for our own past failures to use his gifts aright. We seek now, as a first token of this resolve, to be reconciled to one another as brethren in our Father's house.

We therefore humbly submit ourselves, our Churches and their Ministries, to God, praying that the gifts bestowed on us in our separation may be renewed and increased in full and free communion with one another. We pray that joined so in common obedience to our Lord we may find the way to that fuller unity which we believe to be his will, and proclaim his Gospel with new faith and power and love.

(c) *Then, the Congregation still standing, the Chairman of the House of Laity of the Church Assembly, or other Lay Member of the Church of England, and the Vice-President of the Methodist Conference, or other Lay Member of the Methodist Church, shall read the resolutions of their respective Churches authorizing the inauguration of Stage One, and the text of the resolutions shall be laid on the Holy Table.*

ACT OF PENITENCE

(d) *Then shall the Archbishop of Canterbury say,*

WE COME together in penitence for our manifold sins against God's will and against one another. We confess our prejudice and ignorance, pride and sloth, selfishness and narrowness of vision. We ask God's forgiveness for our past unwillingness to seek reconciliation, and for every refusal to walk in better ways. We acknowledge that through our faults the work of the Gospel has been hindered and the Lord's flock has suffered hurt. We pray that God's forgiveness may bring renewal, reconciliation, and strength to go forth in his name as one body, in unity of preaching and of life, to his glory.

President. O God the Father in heaven,
People. Have mercy upon us.
President. O God the Son, Redeemer of the world,
People. Have mercy upon us.
President. O God the Holy Ghost, proceeding from the Father and the Son,
People. Have mercy upon us.
President. O holy, blessed, and glorious Trinity, three Persons and one God,
People. Have mercy upon us.
President. Remember not, Lord, our offences, nor the offences of our forefathers; spare us, good Lord, spare thy people, whom thou hast redeemed with thy most precious blood.
People. Spare us, good Lord.
President. That it may please thee to give us true repentance; to forgive us all our sins, negligences, and ignorances; and to endue us with the grace of thy Holy Spirit to amend our lives according to thy holy Word:
People. We beseech thee to hear us, good Lord.

President. Son of God;
  People. We beseech thee to hear us.
President. O Lamb of God, that takest away the sins of the world;
  People. Grant us thy peace.

THE COLLECTS

(*e*) *Then the Archbishop shall say,*

> The Lord be with you;
> *Answer.* And with your spirit.
> Let us pray.

Almighty Father, who dost from age to age revive and inspire thy Church: Look now upon us who are here assembled and those whom we represent, and pour upon us thy Holy Spirit to make us worthy of thy calling, that in zeal and courage, faithfulness and love we may manifest thy glory in the service of our nation and the world; through Jesus Christ our Lord, who liveth and reigneth with thee in the unity of the same Spirit, one God world without end. *Amen.*

(*f*) O Almighty God, who hast built thy Church upon the foundation of the Apostles and Prophets, Jesus Christ himself being the head corner-stone: Grant us so to be joined together in unity of spirit by their doctrine, that we may be made an holy temple acceptable unto thee; through Jesus Christ our Lord. *Amen.*

(*g*) *Then a Lesson from the Old Testament shall be read by a Layman of the Methodist Church as follows:*

The Lesson from the Book of the prophet Haggai. God speaks through the prophet of the glorious rebuilding of the temple, an Old Testament symbol of God's presence in the midst of his people, where he is to be worshipped and served.

Haggai 2. 1–9

THE word of the Lord came by Haggai the prophet, 'Speak now to Zerubbabel governor of Judah, and to Joshua the high priest, and to all the remnant of the people, and say, "Who is left among you that saw this house in its former glory? How do you see it now? Is it not in your sight as nothing? Yet now take courage, all you people of the land, says the Lord; work, for I am with you, says the Lord of hosts, according to the promise that I made you when you came out of Egypt. My Spirit abides among you; fear not. For thus says the Lord of hosts: Once again, in a little while, I will shake the heavens and the earth and the sea and the dry land; and I will shake all nations, so that the treasures of all nations shall come in, and I will fill this house with splendour, says the Lord of hosts. The silver is mine, and the gold is mine, says the Lord of hosts. The latter splendour of this house shall be greater than the former, says the Lord of hosts, and in this place I will give prosperity, says the Lord of hosts.'"

(h) *Then shall be said or sung*

Psalm 122

I WAS glad when they said unto me : We will go into the house of the Lord.

Our feet shall stand in thy gates : O Jerusalem.

Jerusalem is built as a city : that is at unity in itself.

For thither the tribes go up, even the tribes of the Lord : to testify unto Israel, to give thanks unto the Name of the Lord.

For there is the seat of judgement : even the seat of the house of David.

O pray for the peace of Jerusalem : they shall prosper that love thee.

Peace be within thy walls : and plenteousness within thy palaces.

For my brethren and companions' sakes : I will wish thee prosperity.

Yea, because of the house of the Lord our God : I will seek to do thee good.

Glory be to the Father, and to the Son : and to the Holy Ghost;

As it was in the beginning, is now, and ever shall be : world without end. Amen.

(i) *Then the Epistle shall be read by a Layman of the Church of England, who shall say,*

The Epistle is written in the fourth chapter of the Epistle to the Ephesians, beginning at the first verse.

I ENTREAT you, then—I, a prisoner for the Lord's sake: as God has called you, live up to your calling. Be humble always and gentle, and patient too. Be forbearing with one another and charitable. Spare no effort to make fast with bonds of peace the unity which the Spirit gives. There is one body and one Spirit, as there is also one hope held out in God's call to you; one Lord, one faith, one baptism; one God and Father of all, who is over all and through all and in all.

But each of us has been given his gift, his due portion of Christ's bounty. Therefore Scripture says:

> 'He ascended into the heights
> With captives in his train;
> He gave gifts to men.'

Now, the word 'ascended' implies that he also descended to the lowest level, down to the very earth. He who descended is no other than he who ascended far above all heavens, so that he might fill the universe. And these were his gifts: some to be apostles, some prophets, some evangelists, some pastors and teachers, to equip God's people for work in his service, to the building up of the body of Christ. So shall we all at last attain to the unity inherent in our faith and our knowledge of the Son of God—to mature manhood, measured by nothing less than the full stature of Christ.

(j) Then shall be sung the following hymn:

1　O thou who camest from above
　　The pure celestial fire to impart,
　　Kindle a flame of sacred love
　　On the mean altar of my heart.

2　There let it for thy glory burn
　　With inextinguishable blaze;
　　And trembling to its source return,
　　In humble prayer and fervent praise.

3　Jesus, confirm my heart's desire
　　To work, and speak, and think for thee;
　　Still let me guard the holy fire,
　　And still stir up thy gift in me.

4　Ready for all thy perfect will,
　　My acts of faith and love repeat,
　　Till death thy endless mercies seal,
　　And make the sacrifice complete.

(Tune: Hereford.)

ACT OF THANKSGIVING

(k) Then shall the Archbishop of York say,

AT this time it is fitting that we should give thanks to Almighty God for the many gifts that he has bestowed upon us through our fathers in the faith, and for the works that he has wrought by them in many generations. We remember before him those who brought the gospel to these islands, those who through the centuries have sought to reform and renew our Church and nation, and all who, by life and good example, have in every generation reflected the glory of God. Especially today do we remember John and Charles Wesley and those who joined with them in spreading scriptural holiness through the land. We thank God for their good works and pray that in our time also the gospel may come home with word and with saving power to those who have not heard or believed that great salvation which is in Christ.

People. O God, we have heard with our ears, and our fathers have declared unto us, the noble works that thou didst in their days, and in the old time before them. O Lord, arise, help us, and deliver us for thine honour.

President. Glory be to the Father, and to the Son: and to the Holy Ghost.

People. As it was in the beginning, is now, and ever shall be: world without end. Amen.

President. We sinners do beseech thee to hear us, O Lord God; and that it may please thee to rule and govern thy holy Church universal in the right way;

People. We beseech thee to hear us, good Lord.

President. That it may please thee to fill thy Church with truth and love, and to grant it unity according to thy holy will;

People. We beseech thee to hear us, good Lord.

President. That it may please thee to give thy Church boldness to preach the Gospel in all the world, and to make disciples out of every nation;

People. We beseech thee to hear us, good Lord.

THE RENEWAL OF THE COVENANT

(l) Then shall the President say,

DEARLY beloved, the Christian life, to which we are called, is a life in Christ, redeemed from sin by him, and, through him, consecrated to God. Upon this life we have entered, having been admitted into that new Covenant of which our Lord Jesus Christ is mediator, and which he sealed with his own blood, that it might stand for ever.

On one side the Covenant is God's promise that he will fulfil in and through us all that he declared in Jesus Christ, who is the Author and Perfecter of our faith. That his promise still stands we are sure, for we have known his goodness and proved his grace in our lives day by day.

On the other side we stand pledged to live no more unto ourselves, but to him who loved us and gave himself for us and has called us so to serve him that the purposes of his coming might be fulfilled.

From time to time we Methodists solemnly renew the Covenant which binds us as it bound our fathers to God. It is right that as we and our brethren of the Church of England come together in reconciliation we should all pledge ourselves to pray and to work for closer unity between our Churches and with all other Christian people. In this intent we bind ourselves with willing bonds to our Covenant God, taking the yoke of Christ upon us.

This taking of his yoke upon us means that we are heartily content that he appoint us our place and work, and that he alone be our reward.

Christ has many services to be done: some are easy, others are difficult; some are suitable to our natural inclinations and temporal interests, others are contrary to both. In some we may please Christ and please ourselves, in others we cannot please Christ except by denying ourselves. Yet the power to do all these things is assuredly given us in Christ, who strengthens us.

Therefore let us make the Covenant of God our own. Let us engage our heart to the Lord, and resolve in his strength never to go back.

Being thus prepared, let us now, in sincere dependence on his grace and trusting in his promises, yield ourselves anew to him, meekly kneeling upon our knees.

Here all shall kneel, and the President shall say in the name of all,

O Lord God, Holy Father, who hast called us through Christ to be partakers in this gracious Covenant, we take upon ourselves with joy the yoke of obedience, and engage ourselves, for love of thee, to seek and do thy perfect will. We are no longer our own but thine.

Here all shall say,

I am no longer my own, but thine. Put me to what thou wilt, rank me with whom thou wilt; put me to doing, put me to suffering; let me be employed for thee or laid aside for thee, exalted for thee or brought low for thee; let me be full, let me be empty; let me have all things, let me have nothing; I freely and heartily yield all things to thy pleasure and disposal.

And now, O glorious and blessed God, Father, Son, and Holy Spirit, thou art mine, and I am thine. So be it. And the Covenant which I have made on earth, let it be ratified in heaven. Amen.

(m) *Then a representative group of Ministers and Lay Members of the Methodist Church shall stand before the Archbishop of Canterbury, who shall say,*

In the name of God who wills that all his people should be one, we welcome you and those whom you represent, into the fellowship of the Church of England, to share and to work with us in the mission to which God has called us all. May he who has given you a good will to serve him grant unto you also strength and power to perform the same. May he accomplish in you the good work which he has begun, that you may be found perfect and without blame at the latter day; through Jesus Christ our Lord. *Amen.*

(n) *Then a representative group of Bishops, Priests, and Lay People of the Church of England shall stand before the President, who shall say,*

In the name of God, the giver of all grace, we now joyfully welcome you and those whom you represent, into fellowship with us in the Methodist Church. May he who knows the thoughts and desires of every heart stablish, strengthen, settle you, and so fill you with all spiritual benediction and grace that you may daily rejoice in his salvation, and be ready to do and suffer his perfect will, that finally you may become partakers of his eternal Kingdom and Glory. *Amen.*

(o) *Then shall the Archbishop and the President stand and the Archbishop shall say,*

Behold how good and joyful a thing it is:
   President. To dwell together in unity.

Then shall they take each other by the hand and say,

Archbishop. The peace of the Lord be always with you:
   President. And with your spirit.

(p) *Then all shall stand, and a Methodist Minister shall read the Gospel, first saying,*

The Holy Gospel is written in the thirteenth chapter of the Gospel according to St John, beginning at the third verse.

   People. Glory be to thee, O Lord.

JESUS, knowing that the Father had given all things into his hands, and that he had come from God and was going to God, rose from supper, laid aside his garments, and girded himself with a towel. Then he poured water into a basin, and began to wash the disciples' feet, and to wipe them with the towel with which he was girded. He came to Simon Peter; and Peter said to him, 'Lord, do you wash my feet?' Jesus answered him, 'What I am doing you do not know now, but afterwards you will understand.' Peter said to him, 'You shall never wash my feet.' Jesus answered him, 'If I do not wash you, you have no part in me.' Simon Peter said to him, 'Lord, not my feet only but also my hands and my head!' Jesus said to him, 'He who has bathed does not need to wash, except for his feet, but he is clean all over; and you are clean, but not all of you.' For he knew who was to betray him; that was why he said, 'You are not all clean.'

When he had washed their feet, and taken his garments, and resumed his place, he said to them, 'Do you know what I have done to you? You call me Teacher and Lord; and you are right, for so I am. If I then, your Lord and Teacher, have washed your feet, you also ought to wash one another's feet. For I have given you an example, that you also should do as I have done to you. Truly, truly, I say to you, a servant is not greater than his master; nor is he who is sent greater than he who sent him. If you know these things, blessed are you if you do them.'

People. Praise be to thee, O Christ.

CONFESSION OF FAITH AND THANKSGIVING

(*q*) *Then shall the Archbishop say,*

Seeing that God has brought us out of our separation into fellowship with one another, let us confess our faith in him with thanksgiving and say,

I BELIEVE in one God the Father Almighty, Maker of heaven and earth, And of all things visible and invisible:

And in one Lord Jesus Christ, the only-begotten Son of God, Begotten of his Father before all worlds, God of God, Light of Light, Very God of very God, Begotten, not made, Being of one substance with the Father, By whom all things were made: Who for us men and for our salvation came down from heaven, And was incarnate by the Holy Ghost of the Virgin Mary, And was made man, And was crucified also for us under Pontius Pilate. He suffered and was buried, And the third day he rose again according to the Scriptures, And ascended into heaven, And sitteth on the right hand of the Father. And he shall come again with glory to judge both the quick and the dead: Whose kingdom shall have no end.

And I believe in the Holy Ghost, The Lord, the Giver of life, Who proceedeth from the Father and the Son, Who with the Father and the Son together is worshipped and glorified, Who spake by the Prophets.

And I believe One Holy Catholic and Apostolic Church. I acknowledge one Baptism for the remission of sins. And I look for the Resurrection of the dead, And the Life of the world to come. Amen.

(*r*) *After which shall be sung,*

> Praise God, from whom all blessings flow,
> Praise him, all creatures here below,
> Praise him above, ye heavenly host,
> Praise Father, Son, and Holy Ghost. Amen.

THE BEGINNING OF THE INTEGRATION OF THE MINISTRIES

(*s*) *Then shall the Archbishop of York read the following:*

NOW that we are reconciled and pledged to seek that closer unity which we believe to be God's will, let us pray that he will bring together our two ministries. One is the threefold ministry of Bishops, Priests, and Deacons, which the Church of England has been careful to preserve, believing it to be God's will that those orders, having come down to us from New Testament times, should continue in the Church. The other is the single ministry of the Word and Sacraments which Methodists believe to have been instituted and exercised in accordance with God's will.

We gladly affirm the reality and spiritual effectiveness of both our ministries. We know that they have, in response to prayer, been blessed and used by God. We wish now to share each in the spiritual heritage of the other and to assure to both our Churches a ministry fully accredited in the eyes of all their members and, so far as may be, of the Church throughout the world.

In the Ordinal and its Preface, which our two Churches have adopted, we have set out our common belief and intention for the ministry in our coming together. It is in the light of this belief and intention that we now pray to God that he will bring together our existing ministries, bestowing upon both the gifts which he has given to each in our separation, and enabling us to go forward in fellowship to the new work which he is giving us to do.

(*t*) *Then shall the books of the ministerial subscription of those taking part be laid on the Holy Table.*

(*u*) *Then all the Archbishops, Bishops, and those Methodist Ministers who are to preside at the local Services shall say together:*

Almighty Father, we thank thee that thou hast blessed us by the power of the Holy Spirit in thy service as ministers in the Body of thy

Son. We thank thee that thou hast now brought together and reconciled these separated members of his Body. We offer ourselves wholly to thee, asking that thou wilt renew in us thy blessings already given, and that thou wilt transcend the differences of our calling and make us one by bestowing upon us what thou knowest us to need for thy service as (Bishops) (Presbyters) in thy universal Church and in the coming together of the Church of England and the Methodist Church.

(v) *Then all shall kneel and sing the following hymn:*

1 Come, Holy Ghost, our souls inspire,
  And lighten with celestial fire;
  Thou the anointing Spirit art,
  Who dost thy sevenfold gifts impart:

2 Thy blessèd unction from above
  Is comfort, life, and fire of love;
  Enable with perpetual light
  The dullness of our blinded sight:

3 Anoint and cheer our soilèd face
  With the abundance of thy grace:
  Keep far our foes, give peace at home;
  Where thou art guide no ill can come.

4 Teach us to know the Father, Son,
  And thee, of both, to be but One;
  That through the ages all along
  This may be our endless song,

  Praise to thy eternal merit,
  Father, Son, and Holy Spirit. Amen.

                    (Tune: Veni Creator, Mechlin Version.)

(w) *Then the Archbishops and Bishops shall kneel, and the President, standing with other Ministers and facing them, shall say,*

The Methodist Church has undertaken that, in following God's call to unity, and in coming together with the Church of England, it will accept for itself the historic episcopate. Today we welcome into our fellowship the Bishops of the Church of England and we pray that God will send the Holy Spirit upon them to guide and strengthen them in the bringing together of the Churches and in the new work which lies before us.

Let us pray.

(*x*) Almighty God, who by thy Son Jesus Christ didst charge the holy apostles to feed thy flock, and didst bestow upon them the gifts needed for that work: Renew, we beseech thee, the blessings already granted to these thy servants whom thou didst call to be Bishops in thy Church, and pour out upon each of them thy Holy Spirit for a fresh dedication to thy service in the coming together of the Methodist Church and the Church of England.

Endue them, we pray thee, as thou didst endue thine apostles, with the fullness of thy grace, that they may be worthy, as true shepherds, to feed and govern thy flock; to offer with all thy People spiritual sacrifices acceptable in thy sight; to preside at the celebration of the Sacrament of the Body and Blood of thy dear Son; and to promote unity and love within thy Church. Grant them such grace, that they may evermore be ready to spread abroad thy Gospel, the glad tidings of reconciliation with thee; and to use the authority given them, not to destroy but to save; not to hurt, but to help. So strengthen them at all times against the assaults of the devil, that whether as rulers over thy household, or as ambassadors for Christ in the world, they may stand ever blameless before thee; and, abiding steadfast in thy service all their days, they may be called at the last, with all thy good and faithful servants, to enter into thy eternal joy, through Jesus Christ, thy Son our Lord, the chief Shepherd and our great High Priest, who is alive and reigns, and is blessed, worshipped, and glorified, with thee, O Father, and with thy Holy Spirit, throughout all ages, world without end. *Amen.*

(*y*) *Then shall the President and other Ministers lay hands on them in silence, after which he shall say:*

We welcome you into the fellowship of the Ministry in the Methodist Church, to preach the Word of God and minister the holy Sacraments among us as need shall arise and you shall be requested so to do. We repeat our pledge that we will serve with you as fellow-workers in Christ and that we will never rest until we have found that fuller unity in him which we believe to be God's will.

(*z*) *Then the President and the Methodist Ministers appointed to preside at the local Services shall kneel, and the Archbishop of Canterbury, standing with four priests of the Church of England, and facing them, shall say:*

Let us pray.

(*aa*) Almighty God, the giver of all good gifts, we praise and thank thee for the ministry of these thy servants, for their faithful proclamation of thy Gospel and their feeding of thy flock. We thank thee that thou hast now called us together as fellow-workers in thy service, and we pray thee to send upon each of these thy servants according to his need thy Holy Spirit for the office and work of a presbyter in thy universal Church and in the coming together of the Methodist Church and the Church of England.

Pour forth thy grace upon them, we beseech thee, O Lord, that within the royal priesthood of thy People they may faithfully fulfil this their priestly ministry. Grant that as true pastors they may watch over the sheep committed to their care, gathering the scattered, bringing back the strayed, and seeking the lost, until they be found. Strengthen them to proclaim effectually the Gospel of thy salvation, and to declare to the penitent the absolution and remission of their sins. Make them worthy to offer with all thy People spiritual sacrifices acceptable in thy sight, and to minister the Sacraments of thy New Covenant. Give them a spirit of wisdom and discipline, that they may show themselves wise in counsel. Make them to be apt and profitable fellow-workers with their brethren in the ministry and with thy chief pastors, the Bishops. Keep them ever blameless in their ministry, so that they, abiding steadfast all their days, may be called at the last, with all thy good and faithful servants, to enter into thy eternal joy, through Jesus Christ thy Son our Lord, who is alive and reigns and is blessed, worshipped, and glorified, with thee, O Father, and with thy Holy Spirit, throughout all ages, world without end. *Amen.*

(*bb*) *Then the Archbishop and the four priests shall lay hands on them in silence, after which he shall say,*

We welcome you into the fellowship of the Ministry in the Church of England, to preach the Word of God and minister the holy Sacraments among us as need shall arise and you shall be requested so to do. We repeat our pledge that we will serve with you as fellow-workers in Christ and that we will never rest until we have found that fuller unity in him which we believe to be God's will.

THE PREPARATION
OF THE BREAD AND WINE

(*cc*) *Then shall be read any notices and biddings for prayer, after which shall be said:*

I will offer in his dwelling an oblation with great gladness: I will sing and speak praises unto the Lord.   *Psalm 27. 6.*

We, who are many, are one bread, one body, for we all partake of the one bread.   *1 Corinthians 10. 17.*

(*dd*) *Then shall be sung the following hymn, and during the singing the bread and wine for the Communion shall be brought by Lay People and placed upon the Holy Table.*

1   Spread the table of the Lord,
        Break the bread and pour the wine;
    Gathered at the sacred board,
        We would taste the feast divine.

2   Saints and martyrs of the faith
        To the Cross have turned their eyes,
    Sharing, in their life and death,
        That eternal sacrifice.

3   Humbly now our place we claim
        In that glorious company,
    Proud confessors of the name,
        Breaking bread, O Christ, with thee.

4   By the memory of thy love,
        To the glory of the Lord,
    Here we raise thy Cross above;
        Gird us with thy Spirit's sword.

5   Guided by thy mighty hand,
        All thy mind we would fulfil,
    Loyal to thy least command,
        Serving thee with steadfast will.

(Tune: Culbach.)

THE THANKSGIVING

(*ee*) *When all is ready the Archbishop and the President together with such number of Bishops of the Church of England and of Presbyters of the Methodist Church as may be needed shall stand at the Holy Table to con-celebrate, and, the hymn ended, the Archbishop shall say or sing:*

(*ff*)   *Archbishop.*   The Lord be with you;
       Answer.   And with thy spirit.
       Archbishop.   Lift up your hearts;
       Answer.   We lift them up unto the Lord.
       Archbishop.   Let us give thanks unto the Lord our God;
       Answer.   It is meet and right so to do.

IT is very meet, right, and our bounden duty, that we should at all times, and in all places, give thanks unto thee, O Lord, holy Father, almighty, everlasting God, through Jesus Christ, thine only Son, our Lord;

Because through him thou hast created all things from the beginning, and fashioned us men in thine own image;

Through him thou didst redeem us from the slavery of sin, giving him to be born as man, to die upon the cross, and to rise again for us;

Through him thou hast made us a People for thine own possession, exalting him to thy right hand on high, and sending forth through him thy holy and life-giving Spirit; for by the gift of that same Spirit thou hast empowered thy People to preach the Gospel among the nations, and to serve thee acceptably as a royal priesthood;

Through him therefore, with angels and archangels, and with all the company of heaven, we laud and magnify thy glorious name, evermore praising thee, and saying,

> *All.* Holy, Holy, Holy, Lord God of Hosts,
> Heaven and earth are full of thy glory.
> Glory be to thee, O Lord most high.

(gg) Then shall the Archbishop, the President, and the officiating Bishops and Presbyters say together,

Almighty God, our heavenly Father, who of thy tender mercy didst give thine only Son Jesus Christ to suffer death upon the Cross for our redemption; who made there (by his one oblation of himself once offered) a full, perfect, and sufficient sacrifice, oblation, and satisfaction, for the sins of the whole world; and did institute, and in his holy Gospel command us to continue, a perpetual memory of that his precious death, until his coming again; Hear us, O merciful Father, we most humbly beseech thee; and grant that we receiving these thy creatures of bread and wine, according to thy Son our Saviour Jesus Christ's holy institution, in remembrance of his death and passion, may be partakers of his most blessed Body and Blood; who, in the same night that he was betrayed, took Bread; and, when he had given thanks, he brake it, and gave it to his disciples, saying, Take, eat; this is my Body which is given for you: Do this in remembrance of me. Likewise after supper he took the Cup; and, when he had given thanks, he gave it to them, saying, Drink ye all of this, for this is my Blood of the New Testament, which is shed for you and for many for the remission of sins: Do this, as oft as ye shall drink it, in remembrance of me. *Amen.*

THE COMMUNION

(*hh*) *Then shall the Archbishop, the President, and officiating Bishops and Presbyters first receive the Communon in both kinds themselves, and then proceed to deliver the same to the other Bishops and Presbyters present, and after that to the People saying,*

THE Body of our Lord Jesus Christ, which was given for thee, preserve thy body and soul unto everlasting life. Take and eat this in remembrance that Christ died for thee, and feed on him in thy heart by faith with thanksgiving.

The Blood of our Lord Jesus Christ, which was shed for thee, preserve thy body and soul unto everlasting life: Drink this in remembrance that Christ's Blood was shed for thee, and be thankful.

(*ii*) *While the People are receiving, hymns and anthems may be sung.*

(*jj*) *When all have communicated the President shall say,*

And now, as our Lord hath taught us, we are bold to say:

People.

Our Father, which art in heaven, Hallowed be thy Name; Thy kingdom come; Thy will be done; In earth as it is in heaven. Give us this day our daily bread. And forgive us our trespasses, As we forgive them that trespass against us. And lead us not into temptation; But deliver us from evil: For thine is the kingdom, The power, and the glory, For ever and ever. Amen.

(*kk*) *Then the President shall say,*

O Lord and heavenly Father, we thy humble servants entirely desire thy fatherly goodness mercifully to accept this our sacrifice of praise and thanksgiving; most humbly beseeching thee to grant, that by the merits and death of thy Son Jesus Christ, and through faith in his blood, we and all thy whole Church may obtain remission of our sins, and all other benefits of his passion. And here we offer and present unto thee, O Lord, ourselves, our souls and bodies, to be a reasonable, holy, and lively sacrifice unto thee; humbly beseeching thee, that all we, who are partakers of this Holy Communion, may be fulfilled with thy grace and heavenly benediction. And although we be unworthy, through our manifold sins, to offer unto thee any sacrifice, yet we beseech thee to accept this our bounden duty and service; not weighing our merits, but pardoning our offences, through Jesus Christ our Lord, by whom, and with whom, in the unity of the Holy Ghost, all honour and glory be unto thee, O Father Almighty, world without end. *Amen.*

(*ll*) *Then shall be said or sung,*

Glory be to God on high, and in earth peace, good will towards men. We praise thee, we bless thee, we worship thee, we glorify thee, we give thanks to thee for thy great glory, O Lord God, heavenly King, God the Father Almighty.

O Lord, the only-begotten Son, Jesu Christ; O Lord God, Lamb of God, Son of the Father, that takest away the sins of the world, have mercy upon us. Thou that takest away the sins of the world, have mercy upon us. Thou that takest away the sins of the world, receive our prayer. Thou that sittest at the right hand of God the Father, have mercy upon us.

For thou only art holy; thou only art the Lord; thou only, O Christ, with the Holy Ghost, art most high in the glory of God the Father. Amen.

(*mm*) *Then the Bishops and Ministers who are to preside at the local Services shall kneel, and the Archbishop and President shall stand facing them. The Archbishop shall say,*

Go forth to the People of our Churches, carry to them the reconciliation begun here today, and charge them in God's Name to unite in fresh dedication to his service;

(*nn*) *The President shall continue:*

And bring together the Priests and Ministers that they may in new grace and new power proclaim the Gospel of the Kingdom, set forth the Word of truth, and offer with all God's holy People gifts and spiritual sacrifices to him in whose Name we bid you go.

(*oo*) *Then shall the Archbishop say,*

The peace of God, which passeth all understanding, keep your hearts and minds in the knowledge and love of God, and of his Son Jesus Christ our Lord: and the blessing of God Almighty, the Father, the Son, and the Holy Ghost, be amongst you and remain with you always. *Amen.*

(*pp*) *Then shall be sung the hymn.*

> 1 Now thank we all our God,
>> With heart and hands and voices,
> Who wondrous things hath done,
>> In whom his world rejoices;
> Who from our mother's arms
>> Hath blessed us on our way
> With countless gifts of love,
>> And still is ours today.

2   O may this bounteous God
        Through all our life be near us,
    With ever joyful hearts
        And blessèd peace to cheer us;
    And keep us in his grace,
        And guide us when perplexed,
    And free us from all ills
        In this world and the next.

3   All praise and thanks to God
        The Father now be given,
    The Son, and him who reigns
        With them in highest heaven,
    The one eternal God,
        Whom earth and heaven adore;
    For thus it was, is now,
        And shall be evermore. Amen.

(Tune: Nun Danket.)

II

THE LOCAL SERVICES OF RECONCILIATION

439 (a) *When the congregation is assembled, the hymn* All people that on earth do dwell (Tune: Old Hundredth) *shall be sung.*

(b) *Then shall the Presiding Minister say,*

WE ARE met together in the presence of God, in order that with his help we may do our part to further in this place the resolve of our two Churches to unite in one Church. We come in thankfulness for his abundant blessings to us, and in penitence for our past failures to use his gifts aright. We seek now to make our own the reconciliation begun in the Service held on . . . . and to come together as brethren in our Father's house.

We therefore humbly submit ourselves, our Churches and their Ministries, to God, praying that the gifts bestowed on us in our separation may be renewed and increased in full and free communion with one another. We pray that joined so in common obedience to our Lord we may find the way to that fuller unity which we believe to be his will, and proclaim his Gospel with new faith and power and love.

(c) *Then, the Congregation still standing, a Lay Member of the Church of England, and a Lay Member of the Methodist Church, shall read the resolutions of their respective Churches authorizing the inauguration of Stage One.*

ACT OF PENITENCE

(d) *Then shall the Bishop say,*

WE COME together in penitence for our manifold sins against God's will and against one another. We confess our prejudice and ignorance, pride and sloth, selfishness and narrowness of vision. We ask God's forgiveness for our past unwillingness to seek reconciliation, and for every refusal to walk in better ways. We acknowledge that through our faults the work of the Gospel has been hindered and the Lord's flock has suffered hurt. We pray that God's forgiveness may bring renewal, reconciliation, and strength to go forth in his Name as one body, in unity of preaching and of life, to his glory.

Presiding Minister.	O God the Father in heaven,
People.	Have mercy upon us.
Presiding Minister.	O God the Son, Redeemer of the world,
People.	Have mercy upon us.
Presiding Minister.	O God the Holy Ghost, proceeding from the Father and the Son,
People.	Have mercy upon us.
Presiding Minister.	O holy, blessed, and glorious Trinity, three Persons and one God,
People.	Have mercy upon us.
Presiding Minister.	Remember not, Lord, our offences, nor the offences of our forefathers; spare us, good Lord, spare thy people, whom thou hast redeemed with thy most precious blood.
People.	Spare us, good Lord.
Presiding Minister.	That it may please thee to give us true repentance; to forgive us all our sins, negligences, and ignorances; and to endue us with the grace of thy Holy Spirit to amend our lives according to thy holy Word:
People.	We beseech thee to hear us, good Lord.
Presiding Minister.	Son of God;
People.	We beseech thee to hear us.
Presiding Minister.	O Lamb of God, that takest away the sins of the world;
People.	Grant us thy peace.

THE COLLECTS

(*e*) *Then the Bishop shall say,*

> The Lord be with you;
> *Answer.* And with your spirit.
> Let us pray.

Almighty Father, who dost from age to age revive and inspire thy Church: Look now upon us who are here assembled and those whom we represent, and pour upon us thy Holy Spirit to make us worthy of thy calling, that in zeal and courage, faithfulness and love, we may manifest thy glory in the service of our nation and the world; through Jesus Christ our Lord, who liveth and reigneth with thee in the unity of the same Spirit, one God world without end. *Amen.*

(*f*) O Almighty God, who hast built thy Church upon the foundation of the Apostles and Prophets, Jesus Christ himself being the head corner-stone: Grant us so to be joined together in unity of spirit by their doctrine, that we may be made an holy temple acceptable unto thee; through Jesus Christ our Lord. *Amen.*

(*g*) *Then a Lesson from the Old Testament* (Haggai 2. 1–9, RSV) *shall be read by a Layman of the Methodist Church, preceded by the following Introduction:*

The Lesson from the Book of the prophet Haggai. God speaks through the prophet of the glorious rebuilding of the temple, an Old Testament symbol of God's presence in the midst of his people, where he is to be worshipped and served.

(*h*) *Then shall be said or sung* Psalm 122.

(*i*) *Then the Epistle* (Ephesians 4. 1–13, NEB) *shall be read by a Layman of the Church of England.*

(*j*) *Then shall be sung the hymn* O thou who camest from above (Tune: Hereford).

ACT OF THANKSGIVING

(*k*) *Then shall the Bishop say,*

AT this time it is fitting that we should give thanks to Almighty God for the many gifts that he has bestowed upon us through our fathers in the faith, and for the works that he has wrought by them in many generations. We remember before him those who brought the gospel to these islands, those who through the centuries have sought to reform and renew our Church and nation, and all who, by life and good example, have in every generation reflected the glory of God. Especially today do we remember John and Charles Wesley and those who joined with them in spreading scriptural holiness through the land. We thank God for their good works and pray that in our time also the gospel may come home with word and with saving power to those who have not heard or believed that great salvation which is in Christ.

> *People.* O God, we have heard with our ears, and our fathers have declared unto us, the noble work that thou didst in their days, and in the old time before them. O Lord, arise, help us, and deliver us for thine honour.
>
> *Presiding Minister.* Glory be to the Father, and to the Son: and to the Holy Ghost.
>
> *People.* As it was in the beginning, is now, and ever shall be: world without end. Amen.

Presiding Minister. We sinners do beseech thee to hear us, O Lord God; and that it may please thee to rule and govern thy holy Church universal in the right way;

People. We beseech thee to hear us, good Lord.

Presiding Minister. That it may please thee to fill thy Church with truth and love, and to grant it unity according to thy holy will;

People. We beseech thee to hear us, good Lord.

Presiding Minister. That it may please thee to give thy Church boldness to preach the Gospel in all the world, and to make disciples out of every nation;

People. We beseech thee to hear us, good Lord.

THE RENEWAL OF THE COVENANT

(l) Then shall the Presiding Minister say,

DEARLY beloved, the Christian life, to which we are called, is a life in Christ, redeemed from sin by him, and, through him, consecrated to God. Upon this life we have entered, having been admitted into that new Covenant of which our Lord Jesus Christ is mediator, and which he sealed with his own blood, that it might stand for ever.

On one side the Covenant is God's promise that he will fulfil in and through us all that he declared in Jesus Christ, who is the Author and Perfecter of our faith. That his promise still stands we are sure, for we have known his goodness and proved his grace in our lives day by day.

On the other side we stand pledged to live no more unto ourselves, but to him who loved us and gave himself for us and has called us so to serve him that the purposes of his coming might be fulfilled.

From time to time we Methodists solemnly renew the Covenant which binds us as it bound our fathers to God. It is right that as we and our brethren of the Church of England come together in reconciliation we should all pledge ourselves to pray and to work for closer unity between our Churches and with all other Christian people. In this intent we bind ourselves with willing bonds to our Covenant God, taking the yoke of Christ upon us.

This taking of his yoke upon us means that we are heartily content that he appoint us our place and work, and that he alone be our reward.

Christ has many services to be done: some are easy, others are difficult; some are suitable to our natural inclinations and temporal interests, others are contrary to both. In some we may please Christ and please ourselves, in others we cannot please Christ except by denying ourselves. Yet the power to do all these things is assuredly given us in Christ, who strengthens us.

Therefore let us make the Covenant of God our own. Let us engage our heart to the Lord, and resolve in his strength never to go back.

Being thus prepared, let us now, in sincere dependence on his grace and trusting in his promises, yield ourselves anew to him, meekly kneeling upon our knees.

Here all shall kneel, and the Presiding Minister shall say in the name of all,

O Lord God, Holy Father, who hast called us through Christ to be partakers in this gracious Covenant, we take upon ourselves with joy the yoke of obedience, and engage ourselves, for love of thee, to seek and do thy perfect will. We are no longer our own but thine.

Here all shall say,

I am no longer my own, but thine. Put me to what thou wilt, rank me with whom thou wilt; put me to doing, put me to suffering; let me be employed for thee or laid aside for thee, exalted for thee or brought low for thee; let me be full, let me be empty; let me have all things, let me have nothing; I freely and heartily yield all things to thy pleasure and disposal.

And now, O glorious and blessed God, Father, Son, and Holy Spirit, thou art mine, and I am thine. So be it. And the Covenant which I have made on earth, let it be ratified in heaven. Amen.

(m) Then a representative group of Ministers and Lay Members of the Methodist Church shall stand before the Bishop, who shall say,

In the name of God who wills that all his people should be one we welcome you and those whom you represent, into the fellowship of the Church of England, to share and to work with us in the mission to which God has called us all. May he who has given you a good will to serve him grant unto you also strength and power to perform the same. May he accomplish in you the good work which he has begun, that you may be found perfect and without blame at the latter day; through Jesus Christ our Lord. *Amen.*

(n) Then a representative group of Bishops, Priests, and Lay People of the Church of England shall stand before the Presiding Minister, who shall say,

In the name of God, the giver of all grace, we now joyfully welcome you and those whom you represent, into fellowship with us in the

Methodist Church. May he who knows the thoughts and desires of every heart stablish, strengthen, settle you, and so fill you with all spiritual benediction and grace that you may daily rejoice in his salvation, and be ready to do and suffer his perfect will, that finally you may become partakers of his eternal Kingdom and Glory. *Amen*.

(*o*) *Then shall the Bishop and the Presiding Minister stand and the Bishop shall say,*

Behold how good and joyful a thing it is:
Presiding Minister. To dwell together in unity.

Then shall they take each other by the hand and say,

Bishop.   The peace of the Lord be always with you:
Presiding Minister. And with your spirit.

(*p*) *Then all shall stand, and a Methodist Minister shall read the Gospel* (John 13. 3–17, RSV), *first saying,*

The Holy Gospel is written in the thirteenth chapter of the Gospel according to St John, beginning at the third verse.
            People. Glory be to thee, O Lord.

After which the People shall say:

            Praise be to thee, O Christ.

CONFESSION OF FAITH AND THANKSGIVING

(*q*) *Then shall the Bishop say,*

SEEING that God has brought us out of our separation into fellowship with one another, let us confess our faith in him with thanksgiving and say,

            The Nicene Creed

(*r*) *After which shall be sung,*

            Praise God, from whom all blessings flow,
            Praise him, all creatures here below,
            Praise him above, ye heavenly host,
            Praise Father, Son, and Holy Ghost. Amen.

THE BRINGING TOGETHER
OF THE MINISTRIES

(s) Then shall be read the following:

NOW that we are reconciled and pledged to seek that closer unity which we believe to be God's will, let us pray that he will bring together our two ministries. One is the threefold ministry of Bishops, Priests, and Deacons, which the Church of England has been careful to preserve, believing it to be God's will that those orders, having come down to us from New Testament times, should continue in the Church. The other is the single ministry of the Word and Sacraments which Methodists believe to have been instituted and exercised in accordance with God's will.

We gladly affirm the reality and spiritual effectiveness of both our ministries. We know that they have, in response to prayer, been blessed and used by God. We wish now to share each in the spiritual heritage of the other and to assure to both our Churches a ministry fully accredited in the eyes of all their members and, so far as may be, of the Church throughout the world.

In the Ordinal and its Preface, which our two Churches have adopted, we have set out our common belief and intention for the ministry in our coming together. It is in the light of this belief and intention that we now pray to God that he will bring together our existing ministries, bestowing upon both the gifts which he has given to each in our separation, and enabling us to go forward in fellowship to the new work which he is giving us to do.

(t) Then shall the books of the ministerial subscription of those taking part be laid on the Holy Table.

(u) Then the Priests of the Church of England and the Methodist Ministers shall say together:

Almighty Father, we thank thee that thou hast blessed us by the power of the Holy Spirit in thy service as ministers in the Body of thy Son. We thank thee that thou hast now brought together and reconciled these separated members of his Body. We offer ourselves wholly to thee, asking that thou wilt renew in us thy blessings already given, and that thou wilt transcend the differences of our calling and make us one by bestowing upon us what thou knowest us to need for thy service as Presbyters in thy universal Church and in the coming together of the Church of England and the Methodist Church.

(v) Then all shall kneel and sing the hymn Come, Holy Ghost, our souls inspire *(Tune: Veni Creator, Mechlin Version).*

(*w*) *Then the Priests of the Church of England shall kneel, and the Presiding Minister, standing with other Ministers and facing them, shall say,*

Let us pray.

(*x*) O God our Father, who hast redeemed us in Christ Jesus and given us a place in the fellowship of thy Spirit and of thy Church, we praise and glorify thy Name for the calling of these thy servants, now to be our fellow-workers. Send thy Holy Spirit upon them, each according to his need, that in the office of Presbyter in thy Church, in the coming together of the Methodist Church and the Church of England, they may serve thee acceptably. Strengthen them that with us they may bear witness to the Gospel of thy universal grace, to the gift of assurance by the Holy Spirit and to the power of that same Spirit to make us perfect in love.

Pour forth thy grace upon them, we beseech thee, O Lord, that within the royal priesthood of thy People they may faithfully fulfil this their priestly ministry. Grant that, as true pastors, they may watch over the sheep committed to their care, gathering the scattered, bringing back the strayed, and seeking the lost, until they be found. Strengthen them to proclaim effectually the Gospel of thy salvation, and to declare to the penitent the absolution and remission of their sins. Make them worthy to offer with all thy People spiritual sacrifices acceptable in thy sight, and to minister the Sacraments of thy New Covenant. Give them a spirit of wisdom and discipline, that they may show themselves wise in counsel. Make them to be apt and profitable fellow-workers with their brethren in the ministry and with thy chief pastors, the Bishops. Keep them ever blameless in their ministry, so that they, abiding steadfast all their days, may be called at the last, with all thy good and faithful servants, to enter into thy eternal joy, through Jesus Christ thy Son our Lord, who is alive and reigns and is blessed, worshipped, and glorified, with thee, O Father, and with thy Holy Spirit, throughout all ages, world without end. *Amen.*

(*y*) *Then shall the Presiding Minister and other Ministers lay hands on them in silence, after which he shall say:*

We welcome you into the fellowship of the Ministry in the Methodist Church, to preach the Word of God and minister the holy Sacraments among us as need shall arise and you shall be requested so to do. We repeat our pledge that we will serve with you as fellow-workers in Christ and that we will never rest until we have found that fuller unity in him which we believe to be God's will.

173

(*z*) *Then the Methodist Ministers (excepting the Presiding Minister) shall kneel. The Bishop and four priests of the Church of England shall stand facing them, and the Bishop shall say:*

Let us pray.

(*aa*) Almighty God, the giver of all good gifts, we praise and thank thee for the ministry of these thy servants, for their faithful proclamation of thy Gospel and their feeding of thy flock. We thank thee that thou hast now called us together as fellow-workers in thy service, and we pray thee to send upon each of these thy servants, according to his need, thy Holy Spirit for the office and work of a Presbyter in thy universal Church and in the coming together of the Methodist Church and the Church of England.

Pour forth thy grace upon them, we beseech thee, O Lord, that within the royal priesthood of thy People they may faithfully fulfil this their priestly ministry. Grant that, as true pastors, they may watch over the sheep committed to their care, gathering the scattered, bringing back the strayed, and seeking the lost, until they be found. Strengthen them to proclaim effectually the Gospel of thy salvation, and to declare to the penitent the absolution and remission of their sins. Make them worthy to offer with all thy People spiritual sacrifices acceptable in thy sight, and to minister the Sacraments of thy New Covenant. Give them a spirit of wisdom and discipline, that they may show themselves wise in counsel. Make them to be apt and profitable fellow-workers with their brethren in the ministry and with thy chief pastors, the Bishops. Keep them ever blameless in their ministry, so that they, abiding steadfast all their days, may be called at the last, with all thy good and faithful servants, to enter into thy eternal joy, through Jesus Christ thy Son our Lord, who is alive and reigns and is blessed, worshipped, and glorified, with thee, O Father, and with thy Holy Spirit, throughout all ages, world without end. *Amen.*

(*bb*) *Then the Bishop and the four priests shall lay hands on them in silence, after which he shall say:*

We welcome you into the fellowship of the Ministry in the Church of England, to preach the Word of God and minister the holy Sacraments among us as need shall arise and you shall be requested so to do. We repeat our pledge that we will serve with you as fellow-workers in Christ and that we will never rest until we have found that fuller unity in him which we believe to be God's will.

THE PREPARATION
OF THE BREAD AND WINE

(*cc*) *Then shall be read any notices and biddings for prayer, after which shall be said:*

I will offer in his dwelling an oblation with great gladness: I will sing and speak praises unto the Lord.   *Psalm 27. 6.*

We, who are many, are one bread, one body, for we all partake of the one bread.   *1 Corinthians 10. 17.*

(*dd*) *Then shall be sung the hymn* Spread the table of the Lord (Tune: Culbach), *and during the singing the bread and wine for the Communion shall be brought by Lay People and placed upon the Holy Table.*

THE THANKSGIVING

(*ee*) *When all is ready the Bishop and the Presiding Minister together with such number of Presbyters of the Church of England and of the Methodist Church as may be needed shall stand at the Holy Table to con-celebrate, and, the hymn ended, the Bishop shall say or sing:*

(*ff*) *Bishop.* The Lord be with you;
Answer. And with thy spirit.
Bishop. Lift up your hearts;
Answer. We lift them up unto the Lord.
Bishop. Let us give thanks unto the Lord our God;
Answer. It is meet and right so to do.

IT is very meet, right, and our bounden duty, that we should at all times, and in all places, give thanks unto thee, O Lord, holy Father, almighty, everlasting God, through Jesus Christ, thine only Son, our Lord;

Because through him thou hast created all things from the beginning, and fashioned us men in thine own image;

Through him thou didst redeem us from the slavery of sin, giving him to be born as man, to die upon the cross, and to rise again for us;

Through him thou hast made us a People for thine own possession, exalting him to thy right hand on high, and sending forth through him thy holy and life-giving Spirit; for by the gift of that same Spirit thou hast empowered thy People to preach the Gospel among the nations, and to serve thee acceptably as a royal priesthood;

Through him therefore, with angels and archangels, and with all the company of heaven, we laud and magnify thy glorious name, evermore praising thee, and saying,

> *All.* Holy, Holy, Holy, Lord God of Hosts,
> Heaven and earth are full of thy glory.
> Glory be to thee, O Lord most high.

(gg) *Then shall the Bishop, the Presiding Minister, and the officiating Presbyters say together,*

Almighty God, our heavenly Father, who of thy tender mercy didst give thine only Son Jesus Christ to suffer death upon the Cross for our redemption; who made there (by his one oblation of himself once offered) a full, perfect, and sufficient sacrifice, oblation, and satisfaction, for the sins of the whole world; and did institute, and in his holy Gospel command us to continue, a perpetual memory of that his precious death, until his coming again; Hear us, O merciful Father, we most humbly beseech thee; and grant that we receiving these thy creatures of bread and wine, according to thy Son our Saviour Jesus Christ's holy institution, in remembrance of his death and passion, may be partakers of his most blessed Body and Blood; who, in the same night that he was betrayed, took Bread; and, when he had given thanks, he brake it, and gave it to his disciples, saying, Take, eat; this is my Body which is given for you: Do this in remembrance of me. Likewise after supper he took the Cup; and, when he had given thanks, he gave it to them, saying, Drink ye all of this, for this is my Blood of the New Testament, which is shed for you and for many for the remission of sins: Do this, as oft as ye shall drink it, in remembrance of me. *Amen.*

THE COMMUNION

(hh) *Then shall the Bishop, the Presiding Minister, and officiating Presbyters first receive the Communion in both kinds themselves, and then proceed to deliver the same to the other Bishops and Presbyters present, and after that to the People saying,*

THE Body of our Lord Jesus Christ, which was given for thee, preserve thy body and soul unto everlasting life. Take and eat this in remembrance that Christ died for thee, and feed on him in thy heart by faith with thanksgiving.

The Blood of our Lord Jesus Christ, which was shed for thee, preserve thy body and soul unto everlasting life: Drink this in remembrance that Christ's Blood was shed for thee, and be thankful.

(*ii*) *While the People are receiving, hymns and anthems may be sung.*

(*jj*) *When all have communicated the Presiding Minister shall say,*

And now, as our Lord hath taught us, we are bold to say:

People.
Our Father, which art in heaven, Hallowed be thy name; Thy kingdom come; Thy will be done; In earth as it is in heaven. Give us this day our daily bread. And forgive us our trespasses, As we forgive them that trespass against us. And lead us not into temptation; But deliver us from evil: For thine is the kingdom, The power, and the glory, For ever and ever. Amen.

(*kk*) *Then the Presiding Minister shall say,*

O Lord and heavenly Father, we thy humble servants entirely desire thy fatherly goodness mercifully to accept this our sacrifice of praise and thanksgiving; most humbly beseeching thee to grant, that by the merits and death of thy Son Jesus Christ, and through faith in his blood, we and all thy whole Church may obtain remission of our sins and all other benefits of his passion. And here we offer and preser unto thee, O Lord, ourselves, our souls and bodies, to be a reasonab holy, and lively sacrifice unto thee; humbly beseeching thee, tha we, who are partakers of this Holy Communion, may be fulfilled thy grace and heavenly benediction. And although we be unwe through our manifold sins, to offer unto thee any sacrifice, yet seech thee to accept this our bounden duty and service; not w our merits, but pardoning our offences, through Jesus Christ o by whom, and with whom, in the unity of the Holy Ghost, a and glory be unto thee, O Father Almighty, world without e

(*ll*) *Then shall be said or sung* Gloria in Excelsis.

(*mm*) *Then shall the Bishop say,*

The peace of God, which passeth all understanding, ke and minds in the knowledge and love of God, and o Christ our Lord: and the blessing of God Almighty Son, and the Holy Ghost, be amongst you and always. *Amen.*

(*nn*) *Then the Bishop and the Presiding Minister*

Go forth to the People of our Churches, carry to tion celebrated here today, and charge them in in fresh dedication to his service.

(*oo*) *Then shall be sung the hymn* Now thank Nun Danket).

III

THE CONSECRATION OF
THE FIRST METHODIST BISHOPS

440 The form will be that provided in the new Ordinal, but there shall be a special form of the Presentation, which will include the reading of the resolutions of the Methodist Conference concerning the acceptance of episcopacy and the entry on Stage One with the pledge to seek organic unity.

Terms of Reference

Resolutions of the Two Churches

In the Summer of 1965 the Convocations of Canterbury and York passed the following resolution:

> That the reports from the Dioceses... enable the Church of England to enter into negotiations with the Methodist Church on the basis of:
>
> (a) the reconciliation of the two Churches in a service which includes the integration of the two ministries;
>
> (b) the acceptance by the Methodist Church of episcopacy in continuity with the historic episcopate and the invariable practice of episcopal ordination for its ministers in the future;
>
> (c) a first stage during which the Church of England and the Methodist Church remain distinct but are in full communion with each other, to be followed by a second stage involving the organic union of the Churches.

The Methodist Conference shortly afterwards passed a similar resolution in the following terms:

> That Conference gives general approval to the main proposals of the Report of the Conversations between the Church of England and the Methodist Church... on the understanding that before full communion between the Church of England and the Methodist Church is established [i.e. Stage One] there will be opportunity for
>
> (a) the clarification of any points in the Report the Conference may require in the light of the judgements of quarterly meetings and synods;
>
> (b) the consideration of such amendments submitted by quarterly meetings and synods as the Conference may determine.

The Convocations asked the Commission to examine such questions of doctrine and procedure as needed clarification before Stage One could be initiated. The following matters were among those which came to the Commission at the request of the dioceses:

1 The Service of Reconciliation.
2 Confirmation.
3 Marriage discipline.
4 Use of unfermented wine.

12-2

5 Establishment.
6 Relations with Roman and Orthodox Churches.
7 Disposal of consecrated elements.
8 Relations with the Anglican Communion.
9 The Diaconate.
10 Lay celebration.

The Methodist Conference remitted the following matters to the Commission:

1 The interpretation of the priesthood and the ministry of the local preacher.
2 Open Communion.
3 The use of fermented wine and the disposal of the elements.
4 Relations with World Methodism and the other Free Churches.
5 Any questions arising in Stage Two, such as changes in the Establishment that should be clarified before Stage One is entered, including the participation of the laity in the Councils of the Church, the work of lay preachers, and the Deaconess Order.
6 The appointment and functions of Methodist bishops.
7 Marriage discipline.
8 The legal implications of Stage One and the preparation of such draft legislation as may be necessary.
9 Consideration of the position of any clergy and ministers who cannot, in good conscience, take part in the Service of Reconciliation, so as to safeguard their status without jeopardizing the attainment of full communion between the two Churches.
10 The form of the Ordinal in the two Churches.
11 The status of ministers who have not been ordained under the historic episcopate transferring to the Methodist Church after the inception of Stage One.
12 The lay administration of Holy Communion.
13 The sacrificial aspects of Holy Communion.
14 The theological implications of Infant Baptism, including baptismal regeneration.
15 Clarification of Scripture and tradition in the Report.

To Our Churches

We have taken the task laid upon the Commission to be that of showing how our two Churches can move into a united Church, on the lines laid down in the 1963 Report, without shirking any difficulties or countenancing the notion of the absorption of one Church by the other. We have examined the implications of the Report; we have considered and used the criticisms which have reached us; we have explored the alternatives to the Services of Reconciliation which have been proposed; and the further our work has proceeded the more convinced we have become that the Report offers the right way forward and that God is calling our Churches to take it. If it be said that the scheme proposed is not free from anomalies, we reply that the present division of our Churches from each other, frustrating their work and running counter to the declared will of God, is an anomaly so great that all other anomalies taken together are insignificant beside it. It is in this spirit that we commend this Final Report to the serious and thoughtful consideration of all members and ministers of both our Churches.

ROBERT LONDIN:

HARRY OXON:

GORDON SOUTHWELL

ERIC KEMP

G. B. TIMMS

LIONEL DU TOIT

ROBIN WOODS

GORDON BRIDGE

SUSANNA HODSON

T. A. R. LEVETT

RICHARD ARGYLL AND THE
    ISLES

DAVID ST ASAPH

HAROLD ROBERTS

GEOFFREY AINGER

ERIC W. BAKER

HOWARD A. G. BELBEN

JOHN C. BLAKE

RUPERT E. DAVIES

LESLIE DAVISON

THOMAS LEE

A. KINGSLEY LLOYD

W. OLIVER PHILLIPSON

EDWARD ROGERS

GRIFFITH T. ROBERTS

FREDERICK A. ROWE

PHILIP H. RACE

PAULINE M. WEBB

22 February 1968

A Note by the Reverend Dr J. I. Packer

The Reverend Dr J. I. Packer is unable to sign the Report, for reasons which he has set out in the following Note.

It gives me deep regret that I am unable to sign this Report. I accept its goal of union by two stages, and the majority of its clarifications and recommendations have my support. In particular, I approve the proposed Ordinal, with its preface on the Ministry; the general treatment of doctrinal questions; the proposals for adjusting our Churches to each other, and for their growth together, during Stage One; and the view of the scheme as aiming at the renewal of the national Church for its national mission. But I cannot endorse the Report's central proposal, that full communion between our two Churches should depend on the integration of their ministries as prescribed in the Services of Reconciliation. My reasons are as follows:

1. The laying on of hands with prayer upon all ministers authorized to celebrate Holy Communion in either Church, however suitable it may appear from other standpoints, is strictly superfluous as a condition of full communion. Once our two Churches stand pledged to unite in an episcopal Church, there is no good reason why either should decline to accept ministers of the other as they are, without this further ceremony. The Methodist Church could readily do this, but the Church of England has so far hesitated, because existing Methodist ministers have no organic link with the historic episcopal ministry. But, as the 1963 Dissentient View stated, 'historic episcopacy is completely without foundation in the New Testament' (*Report*, p. 59). That an episcopal ministry has value, other things being equal, as a sign of the unity, continuity, and authority of Christ's Church, is undoubtedly true, but to suspend full fellowship at the Lord's Table on a non-scriptural requirement, this or any other, is sectarian and wrong, I cannot commend or accept a procedure which involves this mistaken principle.

2. The Services of Reconciliation are not the only viable way forward. The Report itself shows this when it recommends that part of the basis for Stage One shall be 'the firm and declared intention that ways shall be found by which at Stage Two no relations at present maintained by either Church will be broken' (p. 53). This recommendation requires the Church of England to envisage the prospect of taking

intact into the united Church present Methodist relations of full communion with non-episcopal Churches the world over, for it certainly cannot be assumed that all these Churches will be under the historic episcopate by Stage Two. But by undertaking that it will, if necessary, enter into full communion with other non-episcopal ministers at Stage Two, the Church of England will show that it would not in principle find it impossible to establish full communion with non-episcopal Methodist ministers now. Certainly, once this undertaking is given, no good reason will remain for regarding Methodist ministers who have not received the laying on of episcopal hands as out of full communion with the Church of England during Stage One.

I believe that the Report overstates the practical problems which the establishing of full communion on the basis of mutual recognition would raise, and that this alternative needs closer examination than it has yet received. I think it involves far less danger of harmful division within the two ministries than the present proposals do.

It should be said that the Commission is not responsible for the difficulties which I find in its Report. They were inherent in our terms of reference. The Commission has done its utmost, but has not been able to remove them. Their continued presence points to a fundamental flaw in the scheme which our Churches provisionally accepted in 1965.

The undoubted need for a union of our Churches, based on truth, makes it imperative to act with all speed to remove the barrier which this fault of principle has set up.

JAMES PACKER

Index

(This index covers Part 2 of the Report only. All references, except where noted, are to paragraphs.)

Act, Enabling, *see* Enabling Act

Ambiguity, 387, 388; *see also* Reconciliation, Services of

Anamnesis, 98

Anderson, the Reverend Professor G. W., 5

Anglican–Methodist Commission: membership of, ix, x, xi; task of, 1–17; terms of reference, 1 n, page 179; *see also Interim Statement (1958)*; *Conversations between the Church of England and the Methodist Church* (1963); *Towards Reconciliation* (1967)

Anglican–Methodist Conversations: assurances exchanged, 31, 155, 156; *see also* Relations with other Churches

Anglican–Presbyterian Conversations (1966), The: quoted, 105

Articles of Religion, Thirty-nine: 33; quoted, 42, 46, 55, 90 n, 242

Baptism: The Administration of, 241–4; Infant, 237–40; Methodist Statement on, 237 f, 243; minister of, 244; and Regeneration, 229–36; *see also* Confirmation; Initiation; Sacraments

Barrett, the Reverend Professor C. K., 5

Bishops: 116, 148, 151 f, 180, 250, 252 ff, 264, 273, 381, 389, 390, 395; Methodist, 113–39, 250, 355, 423; consecration of Methodist, 130, 369, 373, 381; suffragan, 273; *see also* Episcopacy; Ordination

Bonn Agreement (1931), 154

Bright, Dr William, 24 n

Buchanan, the Reverend C. O., 5

Canons, quoted, 22, 186

Canterbury and York, Convocations

of: Proceedings of, quoted, 21, 155, 194, 248, 260 f, 264, 419

Celebration, Lay: 179–82; dispensations for, 180 ff, 217; *see also* Holy Communion

Chairmen of Districts, 249, 262, 355

Church Army, 211

Church buildings, 318

Church, Community, and State, 285–307

Church of England: 108, 293–6; Established, 285–92, 303; formularies of, 33; Schools, 317; and Crown, 294 f, 306 f; and State, 109, 176

Church Relations in England (1950) (*CRE*), quoted, 31, 36, 251 n

Church of South India, 154, 164, 184 n, 275, 430 n

Church Union, Plan of in North India and Pakistan, 111, 164, 255

Class Leaders, 220 f

Common Prayer, Book of, 33, 42 ff, 90 n, 237, 276, 314, 364; Catechism from, 43, 242, 244, 245; *see also* Ordinal

Communion, Holy, *see* Holy Communion

Communities, Religious, 208, 213

Conference, Lambeth: 1920 Appeal of, 42, 364 ff; 1930 Statement of, 115; 1958 Resolution of, 21

Conference, Methodist, 1, 33, 76, 127, 130, 132, 135 f, 140, 155 ff, 159, 188, 189, 243, 246; ex-Presidents of, 130–2; President of, 129–32; Standing Orders of, 262, 265

Confirmation: discipline of, 194, 196, 245–7, 257; joint service of, 248; minister of, 250–5; *see also* Baptism; Initiation

Constitutional Practice and Discipline of the Methodist Church, The (1963) *(CPD)*, 180 n

Conversations between the Church of England and the Methodist Church (1963) *(Report)*, 22, 38, 49 f, 65, 68, 80, 90 nn, 101–7, 111, 118, 141, 158, 229–31, 237, 306

Covenant, Renewal of, 379

Creeds, The historic, 36, 42, 363; *see also* Doctrine

Deaconesses, 180, 181, 202, 212 f, 218 f, 222

Deacons, 198–202, 374; *see also* Probationer ministers

Deed of Union, 33, 43 f, 55, 74, 76, 243

Disestablishment, 296, 304; *see also* Church of England

Dissentient View (1963), quoted, 49, 54, 90, 158, 229

Doctrine: agreement in, 31–48, 437; differences in, 36–8; latitude in exploration of, 39; sources of, 33, 50–5; standards of, 277; statements of, 31, 36, 38, 64; *see also* Creeds; Scripture

Doctrine in the Church of England (1938), quoted, 116, 147

Eastern Churches, 16, 246, 254

Enabling Act, 309–12, 330–7

Episcopacy: acceptance of, 20 ff, 36, 67; liberty of interpretation of, 67; and priesthood, 71 ff; and union, 363–4; *see also* Bishops

Episcopate, The historic: 81–5, 113–18, 137–9, 363; parallel, 28, 160; *see also* Bishops; Ministry; Ordination

Fermented wine, *see* Holy Communion

Fisher, Archbishop Lord, 5

Free Churches, 30, 154 f, 158

Full Communion, 22, 24, 153–64

Galatians, St Paul's Epistle to, 402, 405–6

Hands, Laying on of, 86–9, 150, 152, 246 f, 256, 389, 390, 402–6

Holy Communion: admission to, 242, 245, 257, 314; consecrated elements, disposal of, 183 f; fellowship in, 104 ff; fermented wine, use of, 185–92; inter-celebration of, 163; officiants at, 71, 180, 313, 364, 366 f; Open, 193–6; Real Presence in, 105; sacrificial aspects of, 90–107; *see also* Full Communion; Intercommunion; Lay Celebration; Sacraments

Holy Orders, Women in, 225

Initiation, Christian, 241–58; *see also* Baptism; Confirmation

Intercommunion: relations of limited, 154, 162, 423–9; *see also* Full Communion; Holy Communion

Interim Statement (1958) *(IS)*, 21, 25, 36, 38, 71 n, 111, 115, 116, 117, 424

Jurisdiction, 66, 400 f

Kent, Sir Harold, 330–9

Laity, 206 f, 226 ff

Lay Celebration, 179 ff

Local Preachers, 216 f, 224

Marriage: 259–69, 316, 333; discipline, 260, 266–9; pastoral care after breakdown of, 263 ff

Marriage and the Family—Declaration of the Methodist Church (1939), 260

Mascall, the Reverend Professor E. L., 5

Methodist Church: doctrine of, 33–48, 49–55, 68–77, 91–7; Church courts, 180; Chairman, 131, 132, 250, 265; ministers, 250, 255; Book of Offices, 91, 183, 244; Union Act of 1929, 297; *see also* Conference, Methodist

Ministries: integration of, 89, 362–70, 381, 382; Lay, 203–28; mutual recognition of, 430–6; non-episcopal, 365 f, 404

Ministry: doctrine of, 65–89, 145–9, 362–4; joint training for, 278–84; threefold, 142 ff, 151 f

Ministry, Baptism and Membership in the Methodist Church (1962) *(MBM)*, quoted, 140 n

Nottingham Conference, 29, 282

Observers, 6
Old Catholic Churches, 6, 16, 154, 157
Ordinal (1662): 33, 71, 140; Revised, Draft, 140–52, 369, 382
Ordination: and commission, 151; and jurisdiction, 66, 400; invariability of episcopal ordination, 82; ministers of, 132, 142, 392, 393–5, 396–423; liberty of interpretation in, 67; not repeated, 72, 76, 126, 150; see also Bishops; Episcopacy; Ministry

Packer, the Reverend Dr J. I., 3 n, pages 182 f
Parliament, 294 ff, 307, 330
People Next Door Campaign, 9
Presbyter, 67, 71 f, 144
Priest, 67, 71 f, 144
Priesthood: 38; ministerial, 70–3; of all believers, 45, 74, 76; of Christ and the Church, 68 f; and Ministry, 65–89; royal, 47
Probationer ministers, 180, 198–202; see also Deacons

Readers, 209 f
Reconciliation, Services of: 20, 66, 192, 357–84, 437, 438; aim of, 357–60; alternatives to, 418–36; Central, 371, 378, 387; Local, 372, 378, 381; criticism of, 385–406, 407–17; Intention, 79, 80, 383, 394, 398, 401 (see also Ambiguity); participation in, 78 ff; non-participation in, 167–72, 315, 410
Reformation, Principles of the, 44, 45, 46
Relations with other Churches, 14–17, 153–7, 429, 433
Re-marriage, 261 f, 267 f
Roman Catholic Church, 6, 162, 384

Sacraments, 36, 72, 75, 92, 363; see also Baptism; Holy Communion
Sacrifice, see Holy Communion
Scotland: 349–56, 437 f; Church of, 306; Episcopal Church in, 6, 339, 353; Methodist Church in, 350–2; possible action in, 354–6
Scripture, supremacy of, 50–64; interpretation of, 56–64; see also Tradition
Simmons, the Reverend A. H., 5
Stage One: 20, 48, 156, 160, 163, 165, 169, 171, 173–96, 307, 409; length of, 170, 271, 414, 427; reasons for, 270–7
Stage Two: 156, 160 f, 163, 165, 307, 416
State, 305–7
Synodical Government, Report on, 228, 306 n

Towards Reconciliation (1967) (TR), 1, 4, 28, 34 f, 41, 48, 49–64, 65–89, 90–9, 142, 197–202, 409
Tradition, value and limitations of, 52–4, 55; see also Scripture

Union: organic, 20, 21–30, 111, 112, 414; schemes of, 14, 18
Unity and Mission, 8–17

Vatican Council, Second, Decree on Ecumenism of, quoted, 162

Wales, Church in: 6, 337, 343; Methodist Church in, 341–4; Negotiating Committee, 345–8; study of situation—Anglican–Methodist Union in Wales (1965), 343
Wesley, John, 33 n
Wesleys, hymns of the, 99
Willesden, Bishop of, 5
Women Workers, 214, 222
Worship, experiments in: 275 f; 'liturgical' and 'free', 275, 276